Raped

Memories of a Catholic Altar Boy

Larry Monte Jr.

Dennis Domrzalski

ISBN: 978-0-9817869-6-4

Library of Congress Control Number: 2010938483

Cover by Kyrsten Sanderson

LOGAN SQUARE PRESS
ALBUQUERQUE, NM
U.S.A.

Dedication

To my wife Jean and to our five children, I dedicate this book with love and with tears. I hope that through these words you will come to understand, at least a little, why I have been what I've been all these years. And I hope that you will forgive me.

What happened to me was unspeakable and horrible. But that is no excuse for my actions—the anger, the rages, the withdrawals and, well, everything.

I ran and hid from these things. I should have dealt with and confronted them long ago. I failed to. I failed myself, and, worst of all, I failed all of you. I apologize.

I have learned one thing the hard and awful way: Silence is death. Never be afraid to speak, to seek help and to confront evil.

It is with a broken but hopeful heart that I apologize for my reluctance, for my fears and for my failures.

I am confronting this now, and I pray that through this, we will be healed and live forever more with joy and with love.

It is with bowed head and on bended knee that I humbly ask all of you for your forgiveness. Forgive me, please. Please, please, forgive me.

Contents

	Introduction	ix
	Prologue	1
1	A True Believer	9
2	The Evil Shroud	15
3	Fr. Robert John Smith	21
4	Two More Twisted Priests	49
5	Soul Murder	57
6	A Living Hell—Effects	68
7	The Circle of Destruction	85
8	Institutionalized	97
9	Invaded	107
10	Twisted	116
11	Screwed Again	123
12	Don't be Afraid to Speak	132
13	Warnings and Lies	137
14	It's Rape!	154
15	Defective to the Core	167
16	My Life Saved	175
17	Money, Hypocrisy, Authority and Power	182
18	Rape Through the Centuries	200
19	Look Behind the Curtain	219
20	Healing	236

"The Catholic Church deserves much of the credit for this book, for without the Church, it would never have been possible."—Larry Monte Jr.

Introduction

Larry Monte Jr. has a goal. The Albuquerque, New Mexico, businessman wants to ensure that never again will a child, or anyone else, be sexually abused and raped by a Catholic priest. Never.

Larry was abused and raped by a priest beginning in 1972 when he was an altar boy in Albuquerque. He is telling his story in brutal, graphic and horrific detail in the hopes that the world, particularly Catholics, and specifically the Catholic Church's leadership, will once and for all come to face exactly what sexual abuse is and how it utterly destroys lives.

Larry has shunned the safety and deception of sanitized, clinical and "proper" terms such as "sexual abuse" in favor of simple, brutal, everyday language. The no-punches-pulled truth can be difficult to take, but it alone has the power to horrify and change.

He wants people to know that priest rape is a bomb that shatters the lives of not only those who were abused, but of all the people they deal with thereafter: their mothers and fathers, spouses and children, brothers and sisters, nieces and nephews, aunts, uncles and cousins, and co-workers, colleagues and friends.

Larry hopes that his story will shock, horrify and anger people to the point where they will rise up and demand that the Church hierarchy protect children instead of remaining preoccupied with its own image, bureaucracy and power.

In his dreams he sees the masses rising up, and with an unrelenting and justice-and-change-demanding fury, storming the Vatican's walls, throwing out its vipers, snakes and rapist protectors and returning the Church to its original principles.

He dreams that Church authorities will turn over to civil authorities for prosecution all rapist priests, humbly ask forgiveness of all priest sexual abuse victims, take real steps to help the Church cleanse itself of its filth, and permanently return to the ideals of its founder.

"Love one another," Larry says. "Do unto others as you would have them do unto you, and do the right thing. Make doing the right thing paramount: more important than legal codes, Canon Law, self-protection, image, liability and protecting assets. Stop the legalities. Act like men!"

Larry's story, though brutal, is for everyone: priest sexual abuse victims, true believers, the squeamish, former Catholics, those who unquestioningly follow Church rules, pedophiles and anyone who believes that child rape is wrong and that its perpetrators should be punished by civil authorities, not protected by secrecy and privilege.

At his very core, Larry holds the hope that in telling his story with such brutal honesty he will enable other sexual abuse victims to begin to heal and to walk out of their darkness of shame, guilt and feelings of worthlessness into the light of joy, pride, confidence, health, love and life. He doesn't want anyone to spend thirty-eight years of their lives, as he did, living in daily torment.

"It's not just okay to talk about these things," Larry says, "it is imperative to do so. Only by telling our stories can we destroy the shame and the guilt that has imprisoned us in Hell on earth. Only by telling our stories can we spotlight the rapists and the organization that has protected them and itself for centuries. Only by telling our stories can we return to Christ's basic message: 'Love one another.'"

An altar boy who bought totally into the Church's teachings and who was being groomed for the priesthood, Larry was fifteen when the abuse began. The boy was introduced to cigarettes, pornography, drugs, alcohol and much more at the hands of his self-appointed mentor, Fr. Robert John Smith of Our Lady of the Annunciation Parish.

The physical terror went on for two years. The emotional torment has lasted thirty-eight years and will never end.

For thirty-eight years, the one-time draftsman, police officer and insurance industry executive has wished, prayed for and craved death as a way to end the unbearable pain, anguish, humiliation, shame, guilt and anger that he lives with each and every day of his life.

He has burned himself with cigars, pounded his head relentlessly into walls and metal doors, tried strangling himself with ties, hanging himself with belts, fondled too many guns and yelled and screamed and pleaded for the pain to go away.

Far too many times, Larry has plunged into the darkest and most horrifying thought of all: that God had abandoned him.

The pain hasn't subsided. Not for Larry, and not for his wife Jean and their five children.

Larry's life was ruined the moment the fat, sweaty, smelly, naked Catholic priest wrestled him to a bed in a cheap motel room, ripped his clothes off, stuck his own pale, hairy, flabby, filth-encrusted ass up in the air, spread his cheeks and demanded that the fifteen-year-old boy sexually satisfy him.

Larry threw up, as he did every time the Catholic Church's chosen one plied him with booze, drugs and porn and demanded sex. He vomited, too, when the priest, after having masturbated and stuck his finger up his ass, decided it proper to celebrate the sacrifice of the mass and give the Holy Eucharist.

There is no way to describe the torment, confusion and sorrow that the fifteen-year-old boy felt. He had believed totally in the Church, believed that priests were his link to God, that priests could do no wrong, that they were, in effect, demigods who were better and holier than he was, that he was supposed to trust and obey them, and that not doing so was a sin that would send him straight to Hell.

The priest didn't rape just Larry's body; he raped his mind and spirit and soul as well, and he destroyed the one thing that Larry needed then and now: belief that he is a worthwhile human being and that God loves him.

Larry's wife and children have borne the brunt of his anger, pain, guilt, shame and daily torment, and they are now all victims of the Catholic Church's crimes. Too many times they have seen their husband and father despair, fly into rages, throw furniture, break dishes and statues, and even more frightening, withdraw and wish for death. No amount of rage or alcohol or hours-long, foot-blistering walks could deaden Larry's pain.

Through the years, Larry has felt that he was damaged goods, a piece of rotten fruit and a human being not worthy of anything, especially of life. He is haunted at night by a dark gray, misty, moaning, faceless, smelling-of-death shroud with long, filthy fingernails that he believes is after his soul.

For thirty-eight years, Larry ran from the truth and lived in terror of being found out. He believed that he was at fault, defective to the core and unworthy of life, and he refused to talk about the abuse and his torment.

No more.

Larry has come to see just what it was that happened to him: That he was raped, that the Church protected the rapist, covered up criminal activity and cared more for a raping, pedophile priest and its own image, rules, bureaucracy and power than it did for one of God's children.

Larry was a true believer. He believed that the Church's words were God's words. He believed that priests were God's representatives who were better and holier than he was and that they could do no wrong. He never missed Sunday mass.

No more.

In his thirty-eight-year journey, Larry has come to see the Church, with its Canon Law, rules, pronouncements and ecclesiastical statements as the epitome of hypocrisy, bureaucracy and evil. His unanswered question of why the Church responds as though Canon Law trumps criminal law and doing the right thing in good and decent society is the bane of his existence.

Larry can take no more. Now fifty-two, he has decided to say what "priest sexual abuse" is and means, and how evil acts against one person can compound and destroy a multitude of lives.

He has decided that the only thing for him to do is to give back to the Catholic Church what it gave him.

This book is Larry's love letter to the Catholic Church that treated him like a piece of human garbage and took away all that he believed.

"They gave me the gift and the nightmare that never stops giving," Larry says. "Now I'm giving it back. They say they want to do penance. Part of their penance should be to know and understand exactly and explicitly what happened to me in those cheap motel rooms, and to face up to what happened to the thousands upon thousands of other children who were raped by Catholic priests.

"They continue to lack even the remotest understanding of what the abuse and rapes and their cover-ups and lies and secrecy and failure to fully acknowledge their monumental sins have done to us and how our lives have been permanently ruined. So I'm going to tell them in explicit detail what it was like to be raped in those motel rooms by their priest, and what it has been like to live with that all these years. It is an ugly, vile and profane story, but there's no other way to tell it because *that's what happened to me!* What you read in this book actually happened! It happened to a fifteen-year-old boy, and I don't apologize for telling the truth.

"The Church has long counted on and fostered our shame, guilt and silence in order to hide its sins. I am no longer part of that. I am no longer an accessory to its crimes.

"I've spent thirty-eight years living in guilt, shame and in daily torment. Multiply that by the tens of thousands, maybe hundreds of thousands, of other children who have been sexually abused by priests over the centuries. Add their parents, relatives, spouses, children and friends into the mix, and it's too much pain and shame and torment to even comprehend. It's overwhelming.

"The Catholic Church gave it to me and to all of us, and now, I am giving all of it back to the Catholic Church—all of it from all of us. I want all of them to suffer daily with thoughts of unbearable shame, guilt, worthlessness, self-mutilation and suicide.

"I want them to bear all the pain and suffering that I have felt and that I have inflicted on my family. I want them to bear my feelings that God had abandoned me.

"I never asked for this. The Church gave it to me against my will. Now, all I'm doing is giving back to the Church what it gave to me. The Catholic Church deserves much of the credit for this book, for without the Church, it would not have been possible.

"It's theirs now. I am free of it."

Prologue

Fucked

No Other Way to Say It

Dear Holy Father, Your Eminence, Cardinals and Bishops of the Holy See:

I was fucked by you and your organization, literally—straight up the ass by one of your priests in 1972 when I was fifteen years old.

He also gave me blow jobs. As he used to say, he loved to suck cock.

I also got to watch your man of God, your successor to the apostles, whack off three or four times a night and spew his cum all over cheap motel rooms.

Offended by my language? Think it's obscene?

Well, I was *offended* at being poked by your priest. That was the obscenity. It's an obscenity beyond words that you "holy men" allowed thousands and thousands of children to be raped by priests. It's an obscenity that you moved rapist priests around from parish to parish so they could rape and rape and rape some more. It's an obscenity that you never listened to warnings that your pedophile priests couldn't be cured and should not have been let out into parishes. It's an obscenity that you refuse to turn these monsters over to law enforcement authorities. It's an obscenity that you still refuse to fully acknowledge what you and your priests did to all of us.

If I had a more powerful word than "fucked," I would use it. But there is no more evocative word in the English language. It conveys rape, pillage, degradation, humiliation, debasement, savagery, contempt, dehumanization, filth and a total and absolute lack of conscience, caring and morality.

Dear brethren, that's what your priest and you people gave to me.

I was offended at being threatened by your priest and told that if I ever told anyone that he had raped me, no one would believe my word over that of a priest's. I was offended by his threats that if I did tell he would get my younger brothers. I was offended by the way another of your priests once grabbed me by the balls, beat me up and nearly drowned me in my backyard swimming pool. I haven't liked your cavalier attitude toward the torment that you have caused me and the tens of thousands of other priest sex abuse victims and our families.

I don't know how else to describe those sex acts—they surely weren't love—and you did teach us always to tell the truth. It's time that you and everyone else begin to really face exactly what your priests and your organization have done to people.

So you know, I didn't swear, drink, look at porn or have sex until I met your priest. Your priest, your man of God, gave me all of that, and more. As humble servants of the truth, I know you will appreciate my forthrightness and willingness to share.

I'll tell you later about your stellar Solider of Christ, Fr. Robert John Smith. You remember Fr. Smith, my intermediary to God who kept a duffle bag full of porn magazines, a supply of Schlitz Malt Liquor and smokes he gave me; dildos, vibrators, plugs, a blow-up sex doll; and pills he gave me to calm my nerves and help me perform. I'll share with you how he would masturbate, stick his fingers up his ass and then say mass and distribute the Holy Eucharist.

Of course, you already knew about him when you hired—I mean, ordained—him at age forty-two after he had already had a history of fucking kids.

I'll get to that later as well.

You need to know that thirty-eight years later, you people, your church, your bishops, your cardinals and your Holy See are still violently raping me and the more than 15,000 other kids in the United States—who knows how many worldwide—who were sexually abused and raped by your priests over the decades. You've been debasing us in that you and your hypocritical organization won't take responsibility for the monsters you set loose on us boys and girls; savaging us in that you've tried to keep us silent with your money; dehumanizing us with your twisted and laughable claims that you're being persecuted like the Jews were by the Nazis; stomping on our minds in that you have cared more about your image, organization and pedophile priests than you have about God's children; and spitting on our souls by covering up crimes and harboring criminals. None of you people could have just picked up a phone and called a cop? You've collectively been raping us by brainwashing us into believing that you were our only path to God; humiliating us by holding your authority over believers and the faithful; shaming us by saying that *we've* got to return to the sacraments; demeaning us by turning your organization into a grotesque mutation of Christ's intentions; raping us by putting your interests over ours; and insulting us by refusing to ask for *our* forgiveness.

You fucked us, and you fucked us hard.

This was supposed to be a love letter, but you haven't given me anything to love. The only thing you evoke in me is contempt and hatred. As I go through this, I realize that my instincts when it comes to you are correct. I don't like being angry—I've had too much of it these past thirty-eight years—and so I'm letting it out and giving it all to you.

Actually, though, it is a love letter—to myself, my family and to all Catholic priest abuse victims. We no longer have to hide, lie, keep quiet, feel dirty, be ashamed and feel like we're unworthy pieces of human garbage and that we somehow offended God. We did nothing wrong. *You did.* Get it straight, *you did!*

I didn't used to be this way. You see, I almost became one of you. I'd been an altar boy since the second grade and was being groomed for the priesthood by my parents and your bureaucracy. What a thrill it would have been for Mom and Dad to have had a priest in the family. They talked about it all the time. I remember how they would be so thrilled to see me in my vestments and how they'd brag on me and show me off.

They had Smith and other priests to the house for dinner and holidays. How those priests ingratiated themselves to those two believers, how they controlled them with their personal blessings, condescending attitudes and talk of how my becoming a priest would please God—how Mom and Dad were raising one of God's chosen ones.

Mom and Dad were true believers. They believed that you and your priests and your organization were the only way to God. They believed every word, period, semicolon and comma that your people uttered and wrote. They believed that your priests were sanctified by God and could and would do no wrong or harm. They believed that those priests and bishops had powers, blessings and grace that they didn't and never would have. They believed that those priests were better than they were.

So did I. I believed totally the things you taught; believed in Limbo, Purgatory, not eating meat on Fridays; original, venial and mortal sins; all of the saints and in all of those ecclesiastical messages and Canon Law pronouncements you put out. I revered priests and believed that they were the successors to the apostles. I believed that your priests could and would do no wrong.

After all, how could a successor to the apostles be wrong? How could it be wrong for one of the successors of Christ's chosen ones to stick his dick up my ass? How was I supposed to challenge the Church? How was I to—how could I—challenge God?

I fully understood that the apostles were men; men who attempted to emulate the love of Christ. Where did that break down?

We didn't come up with this priests-are-holier-than-thou stuff on our own. We didn't wake up one morning and think, "There's an almighty being—God—out there who can save my soul and offer me redemption and eternal salvation—without him I'll burn forever—and the only way to him and his salvation is through the Catholic Church and its rituals, symbols, rules, regulations and priests. It is the only true church."

No. You and your people drummed that into our heads. You've been drumming that into people's heads for a couple of thousand years now. You pounded it into my head and I believed it.

I continued to believe it even after your vile, obese, smelly, boozing, pill-popping Smith raped me, and after he told me I'd better not tell anyone. Do you see the confusion? The shame? The vileness? The disgust? The pain? The horror?

A successor to the apostles, a representative of God, a holy man, a member of the only true church, plied me with booze, porn and dope and fucked me. He actually told me that it was all a gift from God that my parents would never let me have, and then he warned me to keep my mouth shut about it.

You would think that if his raping me was a gift from God, he would have wanted me to shout from a mountaintop so all could hear: "Father Robert John Smith just stuck his dick up my fifteen-year-old ass! Joy oh joy oh joy! Let all the world's children and teens come merrily forth so they too can receive this gift from God!"

You people still don't seem to have much of a problem with rapist priests. You talk about being persecuted, about how it wasn't your fault, how it happened long ago, how you had no control over bishops, and about how you need to do penance.

But you've never talked about admitting guilt, calling the cops on these guys, firing people, getting back to Christ's intentions, changing your sick organization, or about our pain, humiliation and suffering and asking us for forgiveness.

You just talk about yourselves and continue to control people with your lies and rules and regulations.

If you want to do penance, here's an idea: Go into those motel rooms with me as a fifteen-year-old with the piggish Smith and have him fuck you up the ass and blow you, and watch him masturbate and spew cum all over the room three or four times a night. And then endure him offering the sacrament of the mass.

If you want to do penance, feel what it's like to be me with a pain, shame, sorrow, humiliation and sense of inadequacy, worthlessness and defectiveness that grows stronger each and every minute of each and every day.

Be me and feel what it's like every day to want to burn your hands and arms with cigars and slam your head into walls and doors so you can crack open your skull, take out your brain and scrub away its filth.

Be me and know what it's like to be unable to sleep at night because when you do drift off, a dark, evil, moaning, faceless, misty shroud that stinks like death comes to chase you and steal your soul with its black, stinking claws.

Be me and know forever what it's like to put a gun to your mouth and have your finger twitch around that trigger so you can blow your tormented brain out and have it splatter in all its bloody, messy, shameful gore on the wall behind you.

Be me and get caught trying to hang yourself with a few belts buckled together, wrapped around a door knob and thrown over the door.

Be me and feel what it's like to be told by your doctors that you've only got a few years left of life because you're so fucked up that your body is pumping out adrenaline and wearing itself out at an alarming rate.

Be me and know what it's like to have tormented your wife and kids with your anger and silence and sorrow and shame.

Be me and feel what it's like every day to want to die.

Be all of us and our families. Live every day with all this garbage you and your priests have given us.

If you want to do penance, do that. In fact, I'm going to help you do your penance. I'm going to take you with me into those rooms with Smith and through everything I've suffered these past thirty-eight years.

I didn't want to do this. I just wanted to forget this horror, end the misery and move on with my life.

But you people won't let me. Every time you make some sick and twisted excuse for more than 5,700 of your priests in the U.S. having raped children, I fly into a rage. You're harboring criminals, and by doing so, condoning child rape. Your people committed crimes and you did nothing. You let them rape and rape and rape some more. Oh, how you let them rape children!

Every time you obfuscate and hide and excuse and tell us that we must return to the sacraments, it's like you're slicing open my body, pouring salt in it and rubbing it in and laughing.

Remember Matthew:

"And whoever welcomes a little child like this in my name welcomes me. But if anyone causes one of these little ones who believe in me to sin, it would be better for him to have a large millstone hung around his neck and to be drowned in the depths of the sea."

You deserve that millstone—thousands and millions of them—not us.

I'm giving you mine—the one your raping, porn-loving Fr. Smith gave to me.

So many times I've asked God to take all of this from me. The answer I keep getting back—and maybe this is me, not him—is, "Give it to the Catholic Church; it is not me."

You are not him, and so I'm going to help you with your penance by taking you into those rooms with me and Smith.

You will, of course, do your penance as you tell us to do: with shame, humility, true remorse, a rejection of evil, a begging for forgiveness and permanent change.

You will, won't you?

"It is for this class of rattlesnake I have always wished the island retreat—but even an island is too good for these vipers of whom the Gentle Master said—It were better they had not been born—this is an indirect way of saying damned, is it not?"—Fr. Gerald Fitzgerald, Sept. 18, 1957.

One

A True Believer

Dear Brethren:

Mom and Dad were intensely devout Catholics and devoted to the Church. It was typical of their generation and background. Dad's family came to the states from Italy in the early 1900s through Ellis Island. My mother's family came from Ireland.

I'm not sure how they wound up in New Mexico and Albuquerque, but they got here sometime in the 1930s. Dad's father was a bricklayer. Dad graduated from Creighton University and became a mathematician.

The Church was a huge part of our life, and we were always in church. We never missed Sunday mass, and we often made it to mass on weekday mornings. We never missed a holy day of obligation. If there was a holy day, Mom knew about it. We never missed an opportunity when we were *supposed* to be in church.

Mom and Dad thought the Church was a great environment in which to raise us as just, upright and moral kids. It was a tool, and they believed totally in the teachings of the Catholic Church.

I became an altar boy at Our Lady of the Annunciation Parish in Albuquerque shortly after I made my first holy communion in the second grade when I was nine years old. That was the youngest they allowed us to serve, and like a lot of kids from devout families, I jumped at the opportunity because it was the right thing to do.

It was more than that; it was an honor and a privilege at that time to be an altar boy. I was part of the mass, walking and serving with men of God, and, well, to be honest, there was something even better than that: It felt special to be pulled out of class to serve for a funeral or a wedding or a holy day or some other special mass. We even got to get out of class and away from those stern nuns and their starchy habits and angry faces and multiplication table drills!

I would get the six o'clock masses on weekday mornings, and when I did get a Sunday mass, Mom and Dad would always go to it. Sometimes I had multiple masses on Sundays, and Mom or Dad would make sure I got to church.

Mom and Dad were real proud that I was involved in the Church. I remember their conversations about how maybe I or one of my two brothers would become a priest one day and what a great honor it would be to have one of their children answer the "Call." They would talk about what a great honor it was to be part of the mass and to be chosen and selected for that service.

I was proud that they were proud of me. We were raised to please our parents and elders. In those days, kids were supposed to be seen, not heard, and I did my best to live that way.

I was a quiet kid and an okay student. I certainly wasn't genius material and wasn't going to develop new mathematical equations or send rockets to the moon, but I did learn to tie my shoes pretty early on, and I could at least spell my name, so things were all right.

Mom and Dad were strict. You always had to be at dinner, hands and face washed and wearing a clean shirt. As a kid I never went without anything. We always had clean clothes and plenty to eat. I was given the opportunity to get a good education. Mom and Dad were generous people. It was a great way for a kid to grow up. You never talked back or challenged them; that was improper and, well, not just a violation of the rules, but a challenging of their holy parental authority, and a sin.

Your parents have a tremendous amount of influence on you as you are growing up. The Church was part of their life, so it became a part of mine as well.

We moved around a lot. Dad took us to Denver, Massachusetts and to Oregon, and then back to Albuquerque. The first thing we did when we got to a new place was look for a church, and everywhere we went I was an altar boy.

Priests were part of our family. They were always over to the house for dinners and birthdays and holidays, and their presence was always felt. Mom and Dad were very welcoming. Once, in Massachusetts, a priest said mass at our house. What a thrill that was. What a special joy. What a privilege. We were devout and pious and blessed enough to have a representative of God come to our house and celebrate the mass. I felt so special.

There was always talk of one of us being a priest, and I started thinking about it in second grade. I don't know if that's why I became an altar boy, so that maybe I could start on the road to priesthood, or if it was because I became one. All I know is that's when I started thinking of being a priest.

I mean, to be held in that high esteem with the community and the families in the parish. It was Mom and Dad, sure, but also the nuns and the priests. They always used to talk and lecture us about being priests. They had you in school for six hours a day and they would recruit you for six hours. You could never escape the innuendo and the comments; they were always there.

As a kid I believed absolutely in the Church and in the priesthood and in being a priest. I don't ever remember God hitting me on the head and saying, "You're coming." That's not what a calling is. But at a young age I was being mentored, trained and molded, and at that age your mind is so, I don't know, moldable. As I look back on it I don't know how they could do that to a kid, but they did.

They used to teach that the Catholic Church was the one true church. They taught that we were in much higher regard with the Lord than the rest of the people—the rest were pagans. We were the ones that had it figured out. We were the blessed ones. We were the chosen ones. I felt compelled to be part of it. I was raised to believe that there was no greater honor than to serve the Church as a priest and to be called to do that and to say "yes" and to make that special sacrifice. I was even told that I'd have a higher place in Heaven, that there was a kind of ranking up there and that maybe I'd be able to bypass Purgatory.

Priests were the chosen ones, the holy ones who got to consecrate the mass. Their hands and minds were special. They got to touch and bless people. You would take your medals and statues and rosaries to be blessed by the priests. They always had a high status and they were important, more important than the rest of us.

I was a pretty good student. I didn't cause the nuns or lay teachers much trouble—Mom and Dad would not have tolerated it—but that didn't stop me from being occasionally whacked and hit and bounced around by the nuns and lay teachers. I had my ears pulled, and one nun would spout that I was never going to amount to anything. One teacher had a paddle—a baseball bat that he had shaved down and drilled holes into in order to get better air flow so it would hurt more when he whacked you on the ass. He used to brag about his genius for making that paddle, and the pain it would inflict on us children.

I don't remember all the reasons why they hit me, or what I did wrong. Once it was for talking. I remember wanting to ask, "If we're not supposed to talk, why did God give us tongues?" I never did ask it because I knew that if I had, I would have had my tongue yanked out.

Nonetheless, I believed everything. I remember the Church used to teach that if you went to mass nine Fridays in a row, the promise was that God would not let you die alone, that somebody would be there with you when you kicked it. They had all these little rules and teachings, and I believed them all.

I started getting really interested in the priesthood in fifth through eighth grade when we were in Oregon in the Portland area. One summer there I spent a couple of weeks at a seminary kind of becoming indoctrinated to what it would be like to live the lifestyle.

The priests mentored us for two weeks. We were indoctrinated into the silence of prayer and thought and study and what it would be like to live in the dorms, what the food would be like and all of that.

I used to get letters from an outfit in Hays, Kansas, trying to recruit me. They used to write me every week. The letters would always start out, "Dear Brother." They talked about my calling and the need for me to pray and their hope that I was still considering the priesthood and that I would be part of them. I got those letters all through high school when I was at St. Pius in Albuquerque. They kept sending me letters even after I was married.

I do remember my first mass at Annunciation in the second grade. I screwed up big time. I handed over the water when I was supposed to hand over the wine, and I didn't ring the bells correctly. To me those were big mistakes, and the priests then did not have any tolerance for that type of behavior.

I remember screwing up because I was scolded for it in the sacristy by the priest after that first mass. I remember him yelling at me for not behaving appropriately. I was nine years old.

I guess it should have been a warning of things to come.

"I myself would be inclined to favor laicization for any priest, upon objective evidence, for tampering with the virtue of the young. Charity to the Mystical Body should take precedence over charity to the individual."—Fr. Gerald Fitzgerald, Sept. 12, 1954

Two

The Evil Shroud

I'm sure you people sleep well at night knowing that nearly 5,800 of your priests raped more than 15,000 kids in this country and destroyed their spirits and ruined their lives forever. It's a lot more kids than that because that 15,000 number is only those who have filed claims against your bureaucracy. I wonder how many are just so filled with shame, guilt and a feeling of filth that they've refused to come forward and demand justice from your sick organization. Those numbers, by the way, are from your 2004 report on priest sexual abuse in the United States and its yearly audits and amendments.

Some estimates put the number of raping priests at more than 9,000, and the number of abused children in the 100,000 to 200,000 range.

I know you people like to say that it was only 5.3 percent of the 109,649 priests who've served in the U.S. between 1950 and 2009, and that we victims represent a miniscule percentage of the more than 50 million Catholics in this country. You like reducing us to statistics.

Yeah, I'll bet you sleep well—really well, with dreams of happy times and joy and laughter and love. I take that back about love. You can't possibly dream about that. It's not in you.

Well, guess what? We statistics, we miniscule numbers of priest rape victims don't sleep well. I can't sleep, haven't been able to for thirty-eight years now. I can't sleep because when I doze off I'm haunted by evil—the evil that your filthy, stinking, raping priest gave me.

It comes to me at night when I doze off, and it's why I can't sleep and why I can't rest and escape this torment. That's why I get up, night after night, grab a bottle of booze and turn on the TV and drink myself into a stupor. I don't want to deal with it. And that's why I'm dying; dying because my body is tired, worn out and failing; dying because I'm living on adrenaline; dying because it scares me; dying because I am haunted night after night after night.

It stinks—oh God it stinks—and smells like death and it moans and moans and moans and comes after me with its putrid, vile breath, and its long, dark claw-like hands and filthy fingernails. I don't know what it is other than it is evil coming to get me. I can see this thing with these strange arms trying to grab me.

It's eight to ten feel tall and wide and massive. It's like a shroud or ghost-like thing, a dark-gray blanket that's surrounded by a mist. It floats and rides on a mist. It comes up from behind me and hovers over me and moans its sickening, evil moan and starts chasing me. I can barely outrun it. All I can think to myself is that if I trip and fall or get tired and stop running it will get me. I hate it, but it wants me and it won't stop.

I can smell and hear it before it gets to me. Have you ever smelled death? I have. Your evil shroud has that smell, the smell of death. It's a sweet, sickly odor, and I sweat and tremble and scream when it hits my nostrils. It sounds like a freight train getting louder and louder and louder as it rumbles down the tracks towards me.

It's like a dark wet blanket walking through the air, and it won't leave me alone. It upsets my stomach. It makes me sick and scared.

I scream when I hear it and see it and smell it, but nothing comes out—no words, no frantic shouts, no desperate pleas for help, no nothing. Ask my wife Jean. She hears me trying to scream. She says it's like a kid trying to shout for help—a kid who can't get the words out. She says that it's a horrible and eerie sound that I make. I scream and scream and scream but nothing comes out. I scream for help, but no one can hear me. No one can hear me and help me.

When I scream and nothing comes out, your filthy, dark-gray evil shroud moans. It's some kind of guttural moan, kind of like the death rattle, and when I try screaming it knows that I can't alert people to my danger, and its evil moan takes on a snickering tone. It's happy that I can't get help.

It doesn't talk and it doesn't have any facial features, but it communicates. Somehow it has told me that I belong to it. I can't tell if it's man or woman. It tells me that I will never escape, that all my nights will be like this, and that I'm condemned.

Until I wake up and start rustling about, it doesn't leave. That's why I'm so tired all the time. It saps my energy because I'm always trying to get away from it and always trying to stay awake so it doesn't come for me.

That's why I go on long walks. I mean, really long walks—five, six and seven hours at a time. I leave the house and just start walking. I'll go east, west, north, and south, whatever. I don't have any real direction. I just want to walk until I can't walk anymore. I usually do that until I drop. It's upsetting for the kids. I don't leave in a fit of rage or anything, it's just that I have to walk and exhaust myself. I don't know what else to do.

I know that if I get exhausted enough I'll be able to sleep and I won't have to deal with your evil shroud. It'll be there, but it won't be disturbing me because I'll be too damn tired to feel it. That's why I go on those long walks. I walk until I get blisters on my feet and until my feet are sore and red and swollen and in pain. I need that pain. I need it because I'd rather have the pain in my feet—anywhere on my body—instead of in my head. I want this pain out of my head. I just want it gone.

I have to walk. It's better than numbing myself with booze. If I sit around and dwell on this stuff, on that monster, on filthy Smith and those motel rooms, shit, on Schlitz Malt Liquor, I'll go crazy. I'm crazy now. I walk and exhaust myself because if I think about this stuff I know I'll do something that I'll not only regret, but something I'll never come back from.

I know that if I tell somebody that I've got this dark creature following me around, they'll have me committed. I don't know if anyone else sees things like this. It's so real.

My grandfather used to say that it was a sign of a clear conscience if you can sleep. But I don't sleep. I'm always blaming myself and asking, "What did I do wrong? What could I have done differently those days?" And I usually revisit those days and my life and I have found that, well, I have been pretty honorable. I don't lie, cheat or steal. I pay my taxes.

I go over the laundry list and check list and I think, "I didn't just pick up the phone and call somebody a cocksucker." I try to live by the code of being good. I kiss my kids goodnight. I bring my paycheck home. I don't go out and find prostitutes. I give to my charities.

But it doesn't matter what I do. It doesn't matter how good of a life I've lived; it is always there. Your filthy, stinking moaning shroud—the evil you gave me, the shame, the guilt, the feeling that I'm nothing, that I'm rotten to the core, that I'm responsible, that I ruined your priest, that I'm filthy and dirty, that I'm evil—is always there.

It comes ten or twelve times a year. There's no particular time or month. Sometimes it stays two or three nights in a row and then it goes away. My only defense against it is exhaustion and booze.

As I get older it comes more frequently. It's coming more often now. I don't know if that's a sign that it is time for me, that maybe my time is gone, that maybe Father Death is coming to get me. I don't know.

I've had it for years, ever since I was eighteen or nineteen. I didn't have it before your priest raped me. No. Life was good. Life was good and I was happy before your priest raped me! I laughed, felt joy and could cry. I haven't cried since I was eighteen. I didn't see this monster before being raped by Smith! He and you gave it to me.

It came again last night. I was sleeping and I heard a knock at my door, the bedroom door. I thought I was hearing things, and then I thought that someone was in the house. I opened the bedroom door and no one was there. I went downstairs and looked around and out the front door. No one was there.

I went back upstairs and tried sleeping. I heard the knock again. Knock, knock, knock—that damn fucking knock!

I woke Jean up and asked if she had heard the knocking. She hadn't.

"Shit," I told her, "I'm going crazy."

I don't know if I fell asleep or what, but I heard the knocks again, and then, there it was, that sickening, moaning, dark-gray shroud with those claws and that stench chasing me and trying to grab me. It won't leave me alone.

I know what it wants; it wants my soul.

Your evil monster wants my soul!

Well, I ain't going to let it have it. I ain't going to let you have it. I refuse to die—refuse to die for what you and your priest did to me and continue to do to all of us with your lies, cover-ups and refusal to do the right thing.

No, I ain't going to die. I'm going to live, and I'm going to live with joy.

And nothing will bring me more joy than to give all of this back to you—Smith, your monster, the shame, the guilt, the depression, the pain, the suffering, the booze, the sense of worthlessness and the shattered spirit.

I was going to kill this monster, kill it once and for all and get it out of my head and my dreams. That would have been too easy, though, too easy for you.

You have said that you need to do penance, so let your penance be knowledge; the knowledge of what it has been like to be me these past thirty-eight years. Let your penance be torment and sleepless nights and brain-numbing booze sessions in front of the TV. Let your penance be dreams of being chased by an evil, stinking, moaning, ten-foot-tall monster. Let your penance be to smell its stench. Let your penance be to scream for help and not be heard. Let your penance be having to walk until your feet swell and hurt so much that you can walk no more. Let your penance be that it catches you. Let your penance be the torment that I and all of us have been through.

I give up the monster to you. It's no longer mine. It's yours, here and forever more.

You know, I'm really beginning to enjoy giving back to you people.

"We are amazed to find how often a man who would be behind bars if he were not a priest is entrusted with the *cura animarum*."—Fr. Gerald Fitzgerald, Sept. 26, 1957

Three

Fr. Robert John Smith

Dear Holy See and Rapist Protectors:

Fr. Smith loved to play with his balls.

He always used to say how he loved the way his balls felt against the blue velvet seats of the white, four-door, Ford LTDs he would buy. He'd drive around town, or up to Santa Fe, or down to Carlsbad or Socorro or wherever we went, and he'd pull out that Schlitz Malt Liquor and he'd pull his drawers down and yank down his underwear and let his balls rub against the fabric of those car seats, and he'd say how good it felt to have his balls rubbing against that seat fabric.

He'd constantly play with his dick. He'd drive and he'd steer with his left hand and take his right hand and grab my arm and yank it and try to pull my hand onto his dick and his balls. He'd tell me that God created us and our sexuality and how good it was and how good it was to ejaculate and have these feelings and that I needed to experience them and that he would help me experience them. The fat pig—yeah, he was a pig—insisted that I needed to learn how to ejaculate and fuck—that's how he described it—and that he would teach me and that it was all good because God gave us the gift of sexuality. That was always after several malt liquors. He liked whiskey, too. God he loved whiskey. I don't remember what kind he drank, but he kept bottles of it in his duffle bag and he'd take them out and drink right out of the bottle.

He loved porn too. Oh, did Fr. Robert Smith, God's representative on earth, that noble Catholic priest, love porn. He had every porn magazine imaginable, and he kept them in a black duffel bag in the car's trunk or in between the mattress and the box springs of his bed in the church rectory. He'd get that porn out in those motel rooms and get naked and walk his fat, filthy, smelly body around the room and whack off and ejaculate all over the room and on the white towels. He'd do it three or four times a night. One of his favorite things was, as he called it, to measure his load. He'd whack off and cum into a cup or glass and hold it up to his eye and swish it around and exclaim about what a great ejaculator he was.

When I say that Smith would cum all over those rooms, I mean it. He'd spew that shit onto the walls, the floors, the carpets, the bed sheets, the pillows, the furniture and anything and everything else he could hit or drip on.

Not only did he love to measure his load in glasses, your man of God loved to see how far he could, as he called it, shoot his load. He'd lie naked on his back on those beds, whack off and see if he could shoot his cum the length of his abdomen, stomach, chest, neck and head and onto the bed's headboard. He'd whack off in the middle of a room just to see if he could hit a wall with his vile load.

Smith was so proud of his ability to squirt his cum over long distances. He'd laugh like a kid when he'd hit those headboards. The guy really should have been a porn actor. He wasn't clean enough for that, though.

Here's another thing. Your piggish priest never bothered to clean that shit off those walls and carpets and sheets and pillows and headboards. He left it there. That's why I can't stay in hotel or motel rooms.

Smith had dildos, a blow-up sex doll and other toys. He always said he wanted to take me to the porn and sex shops where he got the stuff. Said he wanted me to experience those places and learn about sex. He once told me that when he wasn't hearing confessions, he was in porn shops. I guess that's how much he appreciated God's gift of sexuality. He always got his porn when he was out of town, though. He said he didn't want parishioners to see him in the porn shops in Albuquerque because they were unenlightened and wouldn't understand God's gift of sexuality. I have to, but probably shouldn't, ask, what would the parishioners be doing in those porn shops?

Smith always told me that God wanted me to have these feelings, that God wanted me to smoke and drink malt liquor, and that God wanted me to ejaculate with him.

That was 1972, and I was fifteen years old.

Of course, you guys knew about Smith's perversions, what he claimed as his God-given gift of sexuality and his lust for boys. He was kicked out of a seminary in September 1959 for "molesting" three kids. That was the Christ the King Seminary at St. Bonaventure University in New York State.

You all remember the Sept. 11, 1959, memo from Christ the King detailing how the Springfield, Mass., police told seminary officials about "complaints by some parents against ROBERT JOHN SMITH against whom they made charges that he was guilty this summer.

"The Chancellor ... also stated that the charges seemed to be well substantiated and that Mr. Smith's Pastor is inclined to believe the charges."

That was in 1959! Smith went looking for other seminaries to join, but the people at Christ the King had the sense to tell two of them that he should "never be considered for the priesthood."

That seems strong enough. Never be considered for the priesthood. Never! And yet he came to New Mexico and your people at the Archdiocese of Santa Fe thought he was just what they needed: a raping, dick-sucking, cum-spewing priest. They ordained him in 1971, and a year later, he got me. He got other boys, not just me. He was named in six lawsuits in 1993 and 1994. You settled them. You settled with me in 2007.

You also know that he was housed a few different times at the Servants of the Paraclete center in Jemez Springs, New Mexico. That's where they "treated" pedophile priests from the 1950s on. I'll get to Fr. Gerald Fitzgerald's warnings about "vipers" and "snakes" later. Fitzgerald founded the Paraclete in 1947 and ran it until 1965. You know the irony? He warned you people about your monster priests on Sept. 26, 1957, the day I was born! Read it:

"We are amazed to find how often a man who would be behind bars if he were not a priest is entrusted with the *cura animarum*. Their repentance and amendment is superficial and, if not formally at least sub-consciously, is motivated by a desire to be again in a position where they can continue their wonted activity. A new diocese only means green pastures."

You knew that. You were told. Actually, I think you knew all about Smith and just didn't care about me and all the other kids he ejaculated on and fucked. Tell us all—tell the world. Why did you hire a child molester into an organization that claims to represent God? Why did you put him in a position of authority over everyone, *especially kids?*

I think I know: Yours is a sick, twisted organization, a club that will do anything to protect itself—even if it means throwing children into the garbage dump of life and ruining them for life.

****

Smith was a big, fat, pot-bellied, bald, smelly, sweaty, diabetic.

He used to say he was six feet tall. I think he was only five-ten. He loved to brag about how much he weighed—two-seventy, he used to say. Oh, he was fat and smelly. He would sweat and indulge himself and drink constantly. He'd drive us around in his big white Ford and he'd give us beer and smokes and let us drive after we had boozed. He always wore black pants, and usually a white or navy-blue shirt, white socks and black penny loafers with pennies in the slots.

He smoked constantly and stunk of smoke. His fingers were brown from tar stains. He stunk of BO, bad breath and cologne or aftershave: Old Spice, English Leather and Brut. I still get sick when I smell that stuff, especially Old Spice.

It was early in the summer of 1972 when I met Smith. We had moved back to Albuquerque from Portland. We moved a lot, and whenever we moved to a new place, the first thing Ma and Dad would do was find a church. The nearest church this time—again—was Annunciation.

I continued my service as an altar boy almost immediately after we returned to Albuquerque, and pretty soon after that I met Smith. He was a newly-ordained forty-two-year-old priest, and there was a lot of energy and excitement about him. My first meeting with him was through the mass, and things started getting ugly from there. I was beginning my ninth year of a Catholic education at St. Pius High School. Like my parents, I believed in all of the Church's traditions and teachings. I believed the Church could do no wrong and would never do wrong. I was going to be a priest. That was my foundation and my rock. That was the kid that Smith pounced on.

He was able to ingratiate himself to my family. My parents were devout, and as I said before, they thought priests were God's representatives and could do no wrong. They never thought a priest would hurt a child, let alone give him booze, cigarettes, porn and then rape him.

Smith was always at the house—for weekday dinners, holidays, birthdays, whatever, he was there. He talked about the priesthood and me joining that special, holy group of men. Ma and Dad loved it. They wanted a priest in the family. He won their trust.

They got to know him and they trusted him and that's how he would start maneuvering towards the boys. When he invited me to some kind of mini-retreat one weekend, well, they said it was okay. No, it wasn't just okay, it was incredible for them. They wanted me to be a priest, and here was this priest showering me with attention. I was constantly reminded by my parents and everyone else of what a great privilege it was to have the attention of a Catholic priest.

Did I ever have his attention.

It was in the late summer or fall of 1972 when this all started. Smith took me up to a hotel room in Santa Fe. I didn't have a driver's license yet, but that didn't matter to your priest. He pulled off to the side of the road, let me drive his big Ford LTD and gave me cigarettes.

He said it was okay to smoke because my parents didn't understand kids and would never let me do it. He said what they didn't know wouldn't hurt them. He actually tried to act our age. That's how he got to us. He put himself at our level and talked about how good he was and how he was a great communicator for us kids.

I admit, it felt cool. I was hanging out with a big, forty-two-year-old priest who was giving me cigarettes, letting me eat whatever I wanted and letting me drive a Ford LTD. It was a special treat to go anywhere, but to go somewhere with a Catholic priest, well, that was everything. Being with a priest made it that much more special.

We got to the hotel room and there were two beds and I thought it was pretty cool, but then it wasn't. When we got into the room he went for the curtains and drapes and pulled them closed—he did that each and every time—so that the place was dark. We always stayed in what I call cheesy motels—low-rent places. This one had brown shag carpeting and really cheap art. I remember a lot of those rooms had velvet paintings, which were popular then, and a lot of cowboy art and cheap, mass-produced, Southwestern landscapes.

After closing the drapes, Smith opened his duffel bag, took out the porn, cracked open a couple of Schlitz Malt Liquors, and gave me more smokes—Kools.

You talk about being confused. I'm a fifteen-year-old kid with a Catholic priest, a man of God, and he's got a duffel bag full of porn and he's feeding me smokes and booze. I had never had anything alcoholic to drink before. I had never seen porn before. My parents were pretty straight-laced, and the kids I hung around with were too.

Smith obviously knew that I was scared and nervous because he said I needed to relax. To relax me he gave me another Schlitz. I fell asleep that night in a drunken stupor. Nothing happened that night except the porn, but it led to several more invitations, and every outing got to be more and more disgusting and nightmarish.

The second trip was to Socorro, a small, dusty town in central New Mexico. Smith liked Socorro. He said he liked to get away from his priestly duties because even priests needed to relax. He always found times to get away when we kids would be available, like spring breaks and long weekends. He worked around our holidays and Sundays because we couldn't miss Sunday mass. We could booze, smoke, drive without a license and look at mountains of porn, but we couldn't miss Sunday mass.

We got into the room in Socorro, and to my horror, there was only one bed. The place stunk of Lysol and cigarette smoke. All those rooms did, and to this day I get nauseous when I smell Lysol.

Priests didn't make a lot of money and had to be frugal, Smith told me in explaining why he had gotten a room with one bed. We got into the room, Smith closed the drapes, and out came the porn, the Schlitz, and, this time, some white pills to help me relax. He told me how good porn was and how good it was that I was able to do this and that I needed to explore these things because they were created by God.

"It's okay to look at these women, it's all good," he said.

And then, well, he started denigrating the women in the magazines he was about to masturbate over. Fr. Smith, man of God, let loose. Women were only good enough to suck off a man, he said, and they were only good for men to fuck. Then he started describing them in his terms: cunt, pussy, vagina, knockers, juggs, nubs, melons, bush, fur pie, furburger. He didn't like women's breasts, and he told me how stupid women were. Yeah, stupid. That's what he said.

I didn't think they were stupid. I liked girls. And now, here was this Catholic priest calling them bitches and cunts and furburgers. You think I might have started getting a little confused? You think I might have been horrified?

That porn was good, he said, because God made it all. He told me it was good and that it was good because my parents would never let me experience it.

Then he said he was going to teach me how to ejaculate. For god's sake, I don't know a fifteen-year-old boy in the world who hasn't experienced that, right?

But Smith was going to teach me how to ejaculate, by god. And he tried. He downed some Schlitz and went to the bathroom. The floor had those little square brown tiles and it was sticky. He came out naked with a white towel in his hand, and then he went to it, strutting all over the room. He was, he said, going to beat the meat, flog the bishop and drain the lizard. That's how your priest, your holy man, your man of God talked to me.

The conversation started getting lewder. He started denigrating women again, and then he started masturbating all over the place and on me. It's like he had become possessed or something. I don't know how to describe his look or his demeanor other than that. He masturbated and talked about how good it felt and how good it was and how I needed to try it. He started grabbing my balls. I pushed him away and he got mad.

He started backing off and took on a softer and calmer tone. He told me that this was from God and that because he was a man of God it was a good thing, that it was a natural part of life and that I needed to let go, loosen up and experience it. How else, he asked, would I be able to experience other things in life if I didn't do this?

That all seemed to be contrary to everything I had learned up to that point in my life. I was fifteen years old—a confused young guy—and this Catholic priest had just masturbated all over the room. He was naked and was strutting around the room. Then he went and plopped his bloated body on the bed and told me to come and lie next to him.

I don't even know how I felt except that I was sick and horrified and scared and trembling and ready to throw up. I'm fifteen, and there's a forty-two-year-old man who's basically got me locked in a hotel room, masturbating and pretty much ordering me to do the same. There's this grown man, a man of God who's been handed down an apostolic succession, walking around a hotel room masturbating and spewing sperm all over the room and into those white towels.

What the hell was I supposed to do?

I wanted my parents. I wanted a friend. I wanted somebody to help me. I wanted a priest for god sake. I wanted God. But there was no one there to help; no one to rescue me; no one there to save me; no one to get me out of that nightmare. I was alone and helpless—alone and helpless with your cum-spewing priest.

I couldn't make it work. I couldn't do anything. I was sick. I was alone.

All I know is that I was drunk again. My head was spinning, and Smith was lying there naked. I went to sleep on the floor. Actually, I don't think I slept. How could I knowing the monster was next to me? I always slept with one eye open when I was with Smith.

He tried to be nice on the drive back to Albuquerque. But really, he was just starting to fuck with me. My parents wouldn't understand if told them, he said. No one would ever believe my word over that of a priest's. The porn, the whacking off and his demands that I lie next to his fat, naked body was to be our secret.

Then came the subtle threat. He said he'd like to take my younger brother Jeff on a trip. I knew what that meant, knew it exactly. He'd do the same to my brother. He'd kill his soul as well.

The hint was there. I was to keep quiet and no one was to know, because if I told, my brother would be next. And, I was to continue my sexual education with him—continue it or else.

I can tell you what I did when I got home. I went to the john and puked and then started scrubbing myself with a toilet brush. I felt so damn slimy, so filthy, so damn vile, so worthless, so sick, so confused, so alone, so damn alone with this sick secret. That's how part of me knew this stuff was wrong: I instinctively started scrubbing myself with a toilet brush.

I scrubbed and scrubbed until my arms were raw. I scrubbed my chest and my legs. I wanted to bang my head into something and throw myself into walls. I wanted to hit something, to pound something. I wanted to scream. I wanted to cry. I couldn't cry, though. I haven't been able to cry since then. I can't even cry anymore! I hate this! My god I hate it!

I was living in Hell and I couldn't tell anyone. Who do you tell that a priest has just filled you with booze, pills, smokes and porn and then masturbated all over a hotel room and told you that God wants you to masturbate with him? Who would believe me?

My parents wouldn't have. I'm sure they would have thought I was crazy or possessed by the devil or was just lying. I would have been the one who was wrong. And you know what? I felt like I was wrong. I wish this on no one, not even the vilest pig on the planet: that slow, creeping feeling, that doubt, that shame, that guilt that says you're the one who caused it; that sick, twisted spirit-crushing feeling that says you brought on your own abuse, that you made it happen; that little voice that grows louder each and every day that says you're worthless, that you're a rotten, unworthy human being, that you're a piece of rotten fruit, that you're less than a human and less than a man. I started feeling like I was the one who brought Smith to this—that I had done it.

I wanted out of it. I wanted to die.

Yeah die. Imagine wanting to die and then having the monster who made you feel that way come over to your house! The parents had Smith to the house over and over again. I was insane with terrible and total confusion, pain, humiliation and fear. I dreaded every day. Why was I still alive? Why did I have to continue to go through this? My head was spinning.

There I was, screwed up beyond anything anyone can ever imagine, and Smith was asking the parents if he could take me to a place near Pecos to visit the Benedictine Monastery and do some religious stuff.

How could they have said yes? How could I have let them? How could I have let myself? I don't know anymore other than that I was paralyzed with fear and dread and confusion and shame, and I didn't want Smith to go after my brother. Not Jeff! No, no and no! I could not and I would not let that happen.

And I couldn't let it happen to myself again, but it was coming, and I couldn't do anything to stop it. Just before the Pecos trip, Smith got me in the sacristy at church. I was getting ready to serve mass—I always seemed to draw his masses—and putting on my garments when he thought it necessary to sneak up from behind me and shove his hand up my crotch. He hung on real tight and said he wanted to feel the size of my dick and how things were progressing.

It didn't last but a moment or two, but my god, how was I supposed to go out there and serve mass after the priest had just grabbed my crotch and talked about the size of my dick? How was he supposed to go out there and say mass? How was he supposed to give communion with a hand that had just grabbed a fifteen-year-old boy's dick and balls?

Communion, sex? Sex, communion? How was he supposed to read the gospel and invoke Christ's spirit, blessings and grace with lips and tongue that had just asked me about the size of my dick and how things were progressing?

How? How? How? Somebody please tell me how! Somebody! Where was God?

Smith went out there after grabbing my balls in the church sacristy and said mass and gave communion and acted like a holy man. I wanted to scream to everyone in those pews: "How can you take communion from a fiend, from a deviant, from a monster who just grabbed my balls back in the sacristy? The sacristy! Don't trust him! He's a monster. He's the devil!"

I didn't, though. I should have, but I didn't.

How I wished I had. If I had I wouldn't have gone through thirty-eight years of torment, of insanity, of wanting to kill myself, of keeping one of the Catholic Church's vile, filthy, despicable secrets, of protecting their evil asses. I would have been free of this pain that won't let me sleep.

We started to Pecos, a small village of less than a thousand people in the Sangre de Cristo Mountains southeast of Santa Fe. It's a beautiful place, more than six thousand feet in elevation, near the Pecos River, but for me it was and remains Hell. I think it was in the fall of '72. It was our third or fourth trip, and it was a model for how he operated and how he got to me between twenty and fifty times in those two years.

About thirty minutes out of town he pulled off the road, found a store and bought his Schlitz Malt Liquor and whiskey and gave me smokes and let me drive. He always stopped before our destination to buy booze.

There was a gift shop in Pecos and he bought me a big, giant rosary. It was one of those five-foot-long ones like the nuns wear, and it had huge beads. We were there for some sort of retreat, and he had gotten his room for free, which he was proud of. We got to the room around three or three-thirty in the afternoon. There was only one bed, and that's when all hell broke loose. First he closed the drapes to make the place was dark. How I came to dread him closing the drapes in a motel room!

He popped open the malt liquor, gave me some pills, got out the porn, went to the john and got naked and came out and started prancing his fat, sweaty, smelly body around the room and jerking his joint, as he said, and grabbing my balls and dick. That's when the violence started.

As always, I was scared, wanted no part of it, and was, to put it mildly, reluctant to participate. Smith got furious and yelled at me that I had to loosen up and get on with things.

He threw me on the bed. I wasn't a big kid—I'm six-four now, but then I was five-seven or eight and skinny—and he was two hundred and seventy pounds. He just threw me on the bed. Then he threw himself on top of me—that fat, sweaty, smelly, hairy, stinky, grotesque body. Here was this fat fucker on top of me sliming me up with his stink and sweat and tearing my clothes off. Your priest, your man of God, your successor to the apostles, started ripping the clothes off a fifteen-year-old boy.

I didn't want to give up my clothes. I thought they were the only protection I had from that fat piece of human garbage. But he got them off and rubbed his blubber and his dick all over me. He was pissed that I didn't get an erection.

I was scared and terrified and I kept pleading with him, "Please, let's not do this. I'm not sure I need to understand more." That didn't work, and my first feeling was to kick him in the nuts, but I didn't know what the price would be to pay for that. I was living in fear that if I did hurt him he would get really mad and hurt me back. He was so much bigger than me.

And then I got totally confused. I thought that he was a man of God, one of Peter's successors. I was supposed to obey. No. I was supposed to be accepting because he assured me that he was acting properly because God had given us our sexuality. Here's what he said:

"These things are ordained by God, otherwise we wouldn't be able to feel them. We wouldn't be able to recognize them without God."

He got my clothes off. I still remember his foul breath and his sweat, his stench, his body odor, and I can remember smelling shit and him rubbing his dick all over my body.

That dick-rubbing was a ritual he called "rub-offs." He liked to do his "rub-offs" in the morning after a night of whacking off and fucking me.

I didn't know what to do. He did. He rolled over onto his belly and said I needed to fuck him up the ass because he liked it up the ass. He always said he loved it up the ass. I remember him spreading his cheeks with his hands. I saw his big, brown sphincter and his protruding, slimy red hemorrhoids. That was my first exposure to hemorrhoids ever. He had shit all over his ass. He was not a clean man. It was gross, and to me it was the vilest thing I had, and have ever seen, in my life. Then your good man of God stuck his finger up his ass. He so liked to finger himself in the ass. That, he said, was also from God.

I've seen a lot and I've survived a lot, but I'd rather be thrown onto a battlefield or be left in the desert with a gallon of water and nothing else than to go through that shit again.

I couldn't perform. There was no way I was going to be able to do that. I started yelling and screaming. I guess he got afraid that people in other rooms would hear. I thought if I could find his car keys that I could get out of there. But I couldn't. I was a prisoner. It was as if I had been kidnapped and detained in this hellish, god-awful environment that there was no escaping from. I was trapped.

He gave me more malt liquor to calm me down, and he started making jokes about recruiting me to the priesthood. All I wanted was to go home, but that wasn't going to happen.

He did calm me down, and he started talking to me about sex and how this was stuff that my mother and father would never talk to me about. He said that I needed to work through it and lighten up, and that's when the threats came again.

He said, "Remember, this has got to stay between me and you because I'm part of the priesthood and the apostolic succession." Then he said that I was the one with all the hangups and that I needed to overcome my fears and get beyond them and that he was there to advise me. He told me that I was hung up because my parents wouldn't talk to me about this stuff, and then he said:

"Remember, you've got four other brothers and sisters."

I took that as an immediate threat in that he would go after my brothers and sisters. I think I was astute enough at that age to figure out that I couldn't let that happen. My understanding was that he was going to get them and that I had better comply and get over my hang-ups. He said that I had to remember that our sexuality—and I guess his masturbating in front of a fifteen-year-old and asking to be fucked in the ass—was a gift from God.

"The other kids don't like you," he said. "That's why we've got to get you into the priesthood, and that's why I'm taking you under my wing."

He told me that I'd never have a girlfriend and that I'd never have anything in life unless I did these things with him.

The whole thing must have lasted twenty or thirty minutes. To me it seemed an eternity.

I put my clothes back on—got my jeans on and pulled that belt as tight as it would go—and then, well, it was time for mass. The masses were his way of trying to reassure me that things were going to be okay.

He had a little mass kit that he carried. It had a little crucifix and a chalice and wine and the hosts for communion. He put this stuff on a chair, making a miniature altar, and started to say mass. This time I think he said mass in his boxers. Sometimes he'd be in briefs. Most of the time it was with a white towel wrapped around his bloated, naked body.

You can imagine how fucked up I was then. Smith had just ripped my clothes off and demanded that I fuck him in the ass, and now he was saying mass. The priest who had just molested me was consecrating the wine and the body of Christ!

I was supposed to be doing the readings, and I was so screwed up that I couldn't think. He started yelling at me for not doing things correctly and for not pronouncing the words correctly. He said that mass real fast, sort of a Reader's Digest version of the mass. He always said them fast in those rooms because he wanted to get back to the monkey business. After mass it was time for more malt liquor—the sixteen-ounce cans he always bought, and then, dinner!

The routine was always the same. We'd drive, stop to buy malt liquor, get to the motel around three, and go to the room. He'd get out the porn, pull the drapes shut and then start masturbating and demanding that I fuck him up the ass and that he fuck me. Afterwards, he'd say mass, and then we'd go get dinner.

Dinner was usually a burger and sodas. We'd go to McDonald's or Goody's or Denny's, or a Sonic or other drive-ins. He loved drive-ins. Those were high-class places to Smith. After dinner we'd go back to the room—they were always dark, dingy and smelly—for more malt liquor, pills, porn, masturbation, blow jobs, anal sex and talk of God and the priesthood.

To this day I don't know why I kept going on those trips with the rapist. I don't know why I never said "no!" and never told anyone, other than that I was living in sheer and stark terror. You know what it was like to drive with him and listen to him talk incessantly about masturbation?

Try to picture yourself in a line of kids, and one-by-one, starting with the first, they're being led away to be flogged and beaten. Now imagine that you're third in line. It was pure dread, anxiety and nerves. I was getting ready to take an incredible beating.

It was like this: When we'd start out in the car from Albuquerque, it was like I was third in line to be beaten. When we stopped to get malt liquor, I was second. And when those motel room doors opened, oh, it was my turn to be beaten mercilessly.

I never had time to look at and enjoy the scenery on those drives—those red and barren mesas that flew by. Actually, I had the time, I just didn't have the ability to experience that kind of joy and wonder. I was terrified of what was going to happen to me.

After more of Smith's Godly acts that night, I lay down on the floor and pretended to be asleep, but I didn't dare sleep. Throughout the night he'd get up from his bed and light up a cigarette. Then he'd whack off and ejaculate all over the room again. He'd cum into those white towels. To this day I can't stay in hotels. They make me physically ill.

I can't remember if it happened this time, but it happened often: Smith would be naked and whacking off, and he'd grab one of those clear motel room glasses, hold it up to his dick and cum into it. He was, as he used to say, measuring his load. He was always so proud of himself when he shot what he called "a big load" into those glasses.

The drive back from Pecos was horrifying. Smith was trying to be upbeat and get me into a good mood. He said he wanted to take me to a ball game and to San Antonio, Texas, and Six Flags Amusement Park. Then he tried to take the moral high ground by telling me that I was called to be a priest and a good person and that all that sex stuff was ordained by God and that it was to remain between the two of us.

He talked about secrecy and how the confessional was a secret place, and he said that it was important that I kept this between the two of us and that he wouldn't say anything about it. He was putting it back on me. He said it would discredit me and jeopardize my brothers and sisters. So after that I was constantly in a state of high alert. I didn't want anyone to find out. I was going to take this with me to my grave.

On the drive back in the car, Smith yanked his drawers down and played with his dick and his balls.

Priestly people, kingly people, God's chosen ones

First Smith would say, "The dog is getting ready to fuck." Then he'd tell me through a signal he had. He'd put his index and third fingers tips down on a table, and then he would move his middle, or "fuck you," finger back and forth and rap it on the table.

That was his sign to me to say, "Don't fuck with me. Keep your mouth shut," and, well, "I want you to fuck me."

There were six or seven trips to Socorro, Clovis, Carlsbad, Pecos, Santa Fe and Lubbock. I realize now that he took me out of town to get away where no one would know us so he could have the freedom he needed to fuck. But also, I think, to make me feel lonely and isolated. He knew that I was by myself, knew no one in those towns, and that there was no one I could call for help. The trips are a blur to me because they were so sickening and so horrifying. We'd get to those rooms and he'd take off his clothes and I was supposed to fuck him up the ass. Smith loved to play with his nipples, and he loved to give me blow jobs. As I said before, he used to say all the time how he loved to suck cock.

He told me he had been in the Navy and bragged about his sexual exploits with guys. He also told me of the fun he'd have in sex shops. He had sex in them and told me that if I ever wanted to experience that stuff he would take me to one. As I said, he had a blow-up doll. I never saw him use it. I guess I was his blow-up doll when I was around.

Smith was a fat diabetic who needed insulin injections. He used to make me give him his shots. He always wanted them in his ass. He'd yank off his drawers and bend over or lie on his fat stomach on a bed and I'd see that fat, hairy, slimy, stinky, hemorrhoidal ass and I'd have to stick that needle in his flabby ass cheek. He loved it. I always wanted to puke. It was just another way for him to degrade and use me for his sick pleasures.

I kept serving masses, and I always seemed to get his masses. He got more aggressive about grabbing my nuts in the sacristy.

For me home was a sanctuary, but it really wasn't. I was terrified and sick and could hardly keep food down. I was always throwing up. My parents would ask what was wrong, and I'd say it was growing pains or something and they'd agree. What was I supposed to say? "No mother, I just got fucked up the ass by a Catholic priest." I was afraid of what would happen if I told.

All I could do was try to pretend that all of this hadn't happened and wasn't happening. I worked hard at convincing myself of that. I told myself that it was no one's business, that no one needed to know, that no one would ever know, and that I would take it with me to the grave.

I was feeling dirty and confused and had no idea what to do with myself. I was raised to think that the Catholic Church was held in the highest regard of any institution on the planet. We needed it and its priests for everything; for confession of our sins and for camaraderie and fellowship. You went to them for weddings, funerals and everything. The way my parents and aunts and uncles talked about the Church, well, it could do no wrong.

I lived in constant fear. Who, I thought, the hell is going to believe that the Catholic Church is capable of such activity, and who would believe me?

I couldn't forget it, though, because the parents always had Smith over to the house. He'd greet me with a manly handshake and wink at me, and then, when we were all eating dinner, he'd put his fat fingers on the table and do his "the dog is getting ready to fuck" routine.

Imagine how I felt. There's this priest who is fucking me. He's told me to not tell my parents, and right in front of them and in their house—the people who are supposed to protect me—he's threatening me with his dog-fucking routine. He was abusing me in their presence, and thus abusing them, and he had so much fun doing it. What a sick and twisted human being. What a monster. He was one of yours. He was you.

It seems as if he was at the house every night. He wasn't, but what would you think if the Catholic priest who was fucking you up the ass and giving you blow jobs came to your house? We had a swimming pool in the backyard, and he'd throw his fat, filthy body into it. How Ma and Dad were thrilled that he visited so often. The house was my sanctuary, but every time Smith came in he violated it and he violated me. My safe haven was no longer safe because there was this predator moving about.

One day he took me to his room in the church rectory. He pulled up the mattress and showed me his porn stash, a vibrator and his blow-up doll. How proud he was of his porn, his vibrator and his blow-up sex doll.

All the while, for two years, he kept telling me how all the sex with him was a gift from God and that I needed to look at it from a different perspective. Once he told me that the root of all the evil and problems in the world were because of all the sexual hang-ups people had. He tried to sound like he was on a mission, a mission of saving me from not understanding that in a healthy way. His definition of "healthy" was to rape a young boy, and that a boy's asshole was there to be poked.

On each and every one of those trips, Smith would tell me how he really wanted to invite my brothers with us. Hell, I didn't want that, and I would never let it happen. So it was easier to comply with him as opposed to letting him get his vile paws on them.

Smith loved the Red Raider Inn in Lubbock, Texas. He took me there sometime in 1973. It had been built in 1969 by Texas Tech football star Donny Anderson, and it had the Texas Tech, Red Raider theme. The carpets and the drapes were black and red. There were pictures of a red-caped, masked red raider everywhere. The entrance had a fake, castle turret. He said we were going to go to a football or baseball game, but that never happened. Instead, it was the worst night of my life.

We drove from Albuquerque in his Ford LTD. As we got closer to Lubbock, he started to be stern in the things he told me.

"Now, this is the night when you're going to have to let all of your hang-ups go," he told me. "You'll have to perform. This is going to be a good thing."

After hearing that, my insides turned into a ball of knots. I knew what he expected. The muscles in my stomach and back tensed. I felt like throwing up. I should have just opened the car door and flung myself onto the highway. That would have been better than that night.

We checked into the room. There was only one bed, and I felt sicker. Smith closed the drapes and I felt like puking. He went to the bathroom and came out in his white towel. He got the porn magazines out of his duffle bag and laid them all over the room. He started denigrating women, calling them cunts and describing them in his sick, demeaning, disgusting and vile ways. He hated the female anatomy. He described them that way, and then laughed about it.

He took off his towel and started playing with himself, and that went on for a while. He got on the bed naked and told me that he wanted me to take off my clothes. I didn't want to take off my clothes. "Why do I have to take off my clothes?" I asked.

The answer was the same I'd gotten before. This was a gift from God, that I had to get over my hang-ups and that this was all right because he was a man of God.

"You go ahead. I'm going to go swimming," I said, figuring that was my way of getting out of it. Well, that wasn't going to happen. I went for the door. So did he. Next thing I knew he was standing naked in front of the motel room door, all two hundred and seventy pounds of him, blocking my way. There was this big fat fucker standing in my way. I was trapped.

I couldn't do anything but submit. He started drinking and he gave me some of those white pills. There wasn't anything else to do. We had no food, just Schlitz Malt Liquor. I got so dizzy that I threw up. I don't know what happened the rest of the night except that it was Hell. I don't know if my mind will let me go there anymore. It was the most hellish night of my life.

All I can remember when I think of that night is black and red. Black and fucking red. Those colors haunt me.

Smith was in good spirits on the drive back to Albuquerque. He played with himself in the car and told me I had done well and that I was getting over my sexual hang-ups. I got home and did what I always did after those trips. I went to the john and started scrubbing myself with a toilet brush.

I can tell you exactly how I felt after that. It felt like someone had taken an egg beater to my brain and just whipped, just whipped it all up. I wasn't really angry. I just had this painful fear of being discovered, of being outed, and of being found out. I was confused, upset and disappointed with myself as a person. I hated myself. At that point I didn't feel like I was worthy of anything. I felt like I was some sort of condemned freak and a piece of rotten fruit. I didn't know how I was going to keep everything together.

Then there was a trip to Clovis, a military town of about thirty-thousand in the middle of eastern New Mexico's desolate, red-rock, baked-earth cow country, for the ordination into the priesthood of one of Smith's buddies. I was sitting in the church in the pew watching all those guys up on the altar in their costumes, the Godly, teen-raping Fr. Smith included. I couldn't shake the idea of how many kids all of them together had fucked and blown and cummed on.

They had an overhead projector that kept flashing pictures of priests and holy stuff on the wall, and throughout the ceremony they kept singing: "Priestly people, kingly people. God's chosen ones."

I can't get those words out of my head. To this day they scream at me. I was sitting in the pew by myself, and all I could think about was what was going to happen next in the evening at the motel room after Smith and his pals had inducted some guy into their Let's-Fuck-Boys Club.

I remember thinking that I didn't want anything to do with it. They were in these beautiful and expensive robes with gold chalices all around and beautiful music playing and songs being sung and were making this man part of the church that Peter and Christ founded, part of an elite group of men who were God's representatives on earth, and afterward, at least one of them was going to go back to a motel room to fuck me and to make me, a fifteen-or-sixteen-year-old, fuck him.

My thoughts were starting to get really confused. Confused is so, so too mild a word to describe what was going on in my mind. I was insane. The pig was up on the altar laying hands on a deacon. Even at that age I could recognize that two and two didn't make five. Smith was trying to make two and two make, God knows what, but it was sickening.

I had started reading the scriptures, and I knew that none of this was supposed to be right, that a child rapist should not have been helping ordain a new priest. My thoughts of God were starting to get confused. Where was he? Why wasn't he stopping this? Why wasn't he burning the church down or slaying the rapist, or at least paralyzing him? I felt like I was slowly being taken into their club, and I felt vile, disgusting, lost, abandoned and hopeless.

After the ordination we went to a reception and had punch and cake. Smith and I went back to the motel room, and this is another evening that totally escapes my mind. I'm even totally blank on how I got home the next day.

All I know is that I did get home. It was a weekend and I got home on a weekend night because, God help me, I wasn't allowed to miss Sunday mass because that was a mortal sin. If I missed mass I'd be condemned to Hell. Smith could have me fuck him up the ass and give me blow jobs, and that was okay because God gave us our sexuality, but I'd go to Hell for missing a Sunday mass.

To this day I hate driving through Clovis. I get a shiver up my spine and I want to puke when I drive through that city.

It was all a perfect setup by Smith and the Catholic Church to physically and mentally abuse young boys. They ordain a known child molester, put him into a parish loaded with prey, fill the kids and their families with religious beliefs—especially the idea that they'll all go to Hell if they don't obey the priest's every word—and then let the priest pounce on the kids.

They leave those kids shells, shells without joy and love and with only feelings of evil, shame and guilt.

By this time I was beginning to think that I was a homosexual. Smith certainly wanted me to be one. My head was a mess.

In my senior year in high school we had one last trip, to Carlsbad, New Mexico, and the Holiday Inn. For me it had the potential for even more horror because Jeff was along. Smith said he wanted to show us the Carlsbad Caverns.

We got to the room and Smith excused Jeff out of the room and started his routine. He said it would be better if Jeff was gone. He said, "You know, you don't want your brother, we don't want to bring your brother in on this. We can, but we don't want to do that."

I took that as an innuendo of it was either me or my little brother. Smith got his fat, filthy body naked and started masturbating all over the room like he always did. He grabbed my balls through my pants and kept insisting that I join him in his God-sanctioned sexual activity, but every time he grabbed me I pushed back. I wouldn't have any part of it.

All I can remember is how angry I was. It was the same bullshit. Smith kept saying how these sexual feelings were from God and that I once again needed to explore and experience them. We could work fast, he said, because Jeff would be back. I finally realized that it was all bullshit and I pushed him away and had no part of it.

Smith and I had hundreds of conversations over those years, and I can't think of one that didn't include sex, the joy of masturbation and how I needed to explore those God-given feelings of having sex with him. He once told me that he had spent a lot of time in Chicago after his stint in the Navy, with the Boy Scouts, which now makes me cringe and curse. He told me about all his sexual encounters in the Navy. Yeah, I got to hear all about how many guys he blew. He said he went to a seminary in San Antonio and was ordained in Albuquerque.

Smith, that man of God, once took me up to the Paraclete compound in Jemez Springs. He told me we were visiting one of his friends. I thought it was a retirement home—didn't know that it was a haven for boy-fucking priests. Why would he take a kid there other than to show me off? You talk about leading a lamb to slaughter.

He went inside to visit his pals and I roamed around the grounds. We were there for a couple of hours. Now that I think of it, he and his other raping priests were probably high-fiving each other over the fact that he had a young boy to fuck.

Why would the people in charge of the place let a kid up there? Will somebody tell me that? What was wrong with those people?

I went up there a few other times, once with a gal who I was kind of dating. She went there to visit a priest—her father!

There's one other thing about your Godly Fr. Smith. He was in our house once, in a bedroom. Mom walked in and, well, she caught him whacking off on the bed.

Your man of God was masturbating in and spewing his cum over our house. What a fucking well-adjusted human being.

I must end this, my dearest brethren, by telling you that I forgot one detail. On all those trips that Smith and I took, those trips where Smith got naked, whacked off, spewed cum all over motel rooms and all over me; those trips where he spread his fat ass cheeks and demanded that I fuck him; those trips where he ripped off my clothes; where he rubbed his dick all over me and where he stuck his fingers up his ass before saying mass; where he plied a fifteen-year-old boy with booze, porn, smokes and drugs and told the kid that God wanted us to screw each other; those trips where he ejaculated into a glass to measure his load; those trips where he tried to shoot his load over his body and onto the bed headboards, you know how he began each and every one of them in the car in Albuquerque?

By saying the rosary.

"These men, your Excellency, are devils and the wrath of God is upon them." Fr. Gerald Fitzgerald, Sept. 18, 1957

Four

Two More Twisted Priests

How many of you would like this to happen to you? You're a kid in your backyard swimming pool with a guy who's more than twice your age and he starts wrestling with you. It seems like fun at first, but then the guy starts getting really violent, and then he grabs your balls and squeezes them so you're screaming and knifing over in pain, and then he gets your body and head under the water and keeps you there until you almost drown.

Or how about this: You go to a much older guy's apartment to help him move, and when you're in his bedroom lifting furniture, he lunges at you, throws you on the bed, grabs your balls and says he wants to fuck you.

That happened to me, and guess what? Both of the guys who did that to me were your stellar priests! Ain't that a hoot? Being nearly drowned, and propositioned by Catholic priests when you're sixteen or seventeen years old?

The first was Fr. David Sharp, a Basilian priest who taught math at St. Pius High School in Albuquerque when I started there in 1972.

He was a long-haired guy, kind of a throwback to the 1960s and the hippie movement. He thought he was a real macho guy, I guess. He rode a motorcycle bare-chested and with what I call short-shorts: cutoff denim blue jeans that were cut way too short.

I think he was in his late thirties or early forties at the time. He was strong and he used to like to wrestle with us guys—us fifteen, sixteen and seventeen-year-old kids. He prided himself on being stronger than any high school kid, and for some reason he wanted to beat the shit out of us.

For a while he'd come over to our house for dinner on Sundays. He always wore those short-shorts—why would a guy wear those?—and he used to come to our dinner table shirtless. That always infuriated me because Mom and Dad were strict about attire at the dinner table. My brothers and I were never allowed to come to the table improperly dressed. That meant we had to wear shirts, pants, socks and shoes.

Not Sharp, though.

Now that I think of it, he did that to exert his control and dominance over us. He knew my parents' rule, and he purposely violated it. Give me another explanation as to why he would do that other than he knew he was a priest, that the family adored and revered priests, and that he could use his authority to dominate us and basically shit all over us.

He loved to wrestle Greco-Roman style, and he wrestled with a lot of us. I was basically egged on to wrestle with him by the other guys. It was peer pressure. He would beat the shit out of all of us—slam us to the mat and twist us up like pretzels. He liked to show his dominance over all the boys.

You know how he'd win those matches? He'd grab your balls and squeeze them.

He did that to me twice at St. Pius, in my freshman and sophomore years.

There was one time, though, when he nearly killed me.

He had come over for dinner and swimming and he and I were in our backyard pool. It was good sized pool, fifteen by thirty feet and about six feet deep. He had on those short-shorts, and at one point he started wrestling me in the shallow end. He started getting really violent and throwing me around. Once again, he tied me up like a pretzel, and then, boom, he grabbed me by the balls and squeezed so hard, so damn hard. You can do anything to a man when he's tied up and you've got him by the balls, and Sharp did. He held me under the water until I almost blacked out.

All I remember is hearing my little sister Katie standing by the side of the pool and screaming at him to let me go.

Ask Katie. She'll tell you. Here's what she said: "He used to come over to our house on Sundays and he would wrestle with the boys. He was way too aggressive with the boys. I just know that it was too aggressive, and that it was frightening at times."

That's putting it mildly. It was horrifying. It made me feel powerless and worthless. I guess that's what you people want.

Sharp didn't fight fair; he fought dirty. I hate that cocksucker to this day.

Would you like to have your balls squeezed and then be held under water until you feel like you're going to die? I'd like to know. Do you think that was appropriate behavior on his part? Got any clue as to why I hate your peoples' guts? Any clue as to why I know that the Catholic Church is an evil institution?

No one stuck up for me back then. Certainly not your Church or anyone connected with it. All you did was screw me and throw me into a garbage dump.

You know what Sharp said when he was contacted and asked about this at his home in Wickenburg, Arizona? He said he didn't remember who I was and that we'd have to corroborate this stuff.

I can understand him not remembering me and almost drowning me. He wrestled with a lot of the boys. But I think he would have remembered Katie screaming for him to let me go and me thrashing about in the swimming pool.

There have been times throughout these past thirty-some years when I've thought, "Larry, you're crazy. You're fucked up. You're worthless. You're a piece of garbage. You brought this on yourself." But now I'm beginning to think—actually I thought it back then but I didn't act on it—that a nearly forty-year-old priest wrestling with and beating up boys wasn't right, or that holy, or not what Christ would have done.

****

Let's talk about another of your priestly gems, Fr. Arthur Perrault. He was ordained in Hartford, Connecticut, in 1964, and, isn't this a surprise, by 1967 he was shipped off to New Mexico and the Servants of the Paraclete for treatment as a child rapist.

The Paraclete was opened in 1947 by Fr. Gerald Fitzgerald to treat wayward priests. When it opened in Jemez Springs northwest of Albuquerque it treated mostly alcoholic priests. But things soon degenerated. Here's a portion of a Sept. 10, 1964, letter from Fitzgerald to—I really can't stand these titles, and this one I don't believe—the Most Rev. Joseph A. Durick, D. D., Bishop of Nashville who was in Rome at the time:

"When I was ordained forty-three years ago, homosexuality was a practically unknown rarity. Today it is—in the wake of World War II—rampant among men. And whereas seventeen years ago eight out of ten problems here would represent the alcoholic, now in the last year or so our admission ratio would be 5-2-3; five being alcoholics; two would be what we call 'heart cases' (natural affection towards women); and three representing aberrations involving homosexuality. More alarming still is that among these of the 3 out of 10 cases, 2 out of 3 have been young priests.

"It is very infectious and the prognosis for recovery extremely unfavorable. The majority of psychiatrists, physicians and experienced priests are not sanguine of permanent recovery."

In a Sept. 18, 1957, letter to Archdiocese of Santa Fe Bishop Edwin Byrne, who helped him start the Paraclete retreat, Fitzgerald was brutal:

"For the sake of preventing scandal that might endanger the good name of the Via Coeli we will not offer hospitality to men who have seduced or attempted to seduce little boys or girls? These men Your Excellency are devils and the wrath of God is upon them and if I were a Bishop I would tremble when I failed to report them to Rome for involuntary laicization (removal from the priesthood). It is blasphemous to let them offer the Holy Sacrifice. Experience has taught us these men are too dangerous to the children of the Parish and neighborhood for us to be justified in receiving them here."

Over the years, though, Fitzgerald, motivated by a deep desire to help priests, accepted pedophiles at his center in New Mexico's Jemez Mountains.

For more than two decades he warned bishops and the Vatican that as far as he knew, pedophiles couldn't be cured and that they shouldn't be sent back to parishes.

But they were sent back to parishes, many to New Mexico parishes to prey on our children. New Mexico, in effect, became a dumping ground for pedophile priests.

Between 1992 and 1995, 180 lawsuits and claims were filed against the Archdiocese of Santa Fe. The settlements cost the archdiocese and its insurers $25.3 million in payments to plaintiffs, $4.7 million in attorneys' fees and $1.1 million for counseling.

I was contacted back then by lawyers who were suing the archdiocese and the priests. I was working in Austin, Texas, and, well, I felt too ashamed and embarrassed to join in the lawsuits. I didn't want this out. I had vowed that I would take this sick secret to my grave.

I decided to file an action against the archdiocese in 2007 after reading all your people's excuses and denials. I got a settlement, but I considered it hush money, and that's why I'm now speaking out. The world has to know what priest sexual abuse really is—how vile, sickening, gross and evil it is—and how you people to this day refuse to fully acknowledge your sins, our hurt and ask for our forgiveness.

One of those pedophiles—let's settle on the fact that they're monsters—was Perrault. You know him. When the priest sex abuse scandal broke in New Mexico in the early 1990s, Perrault was named as a defendant in at least four lawsuits. It's estimated that he raped a minimum of ten boys and girls. He fled the archdiocese after he was named in those lawsuits. What a coward. He raped kids and then ran away. A Catholic priest refused to stick around and face the consequences of his evil actions.

I was getting older (probably sixteen by now) and stronger, both physically and mentally, and by the time Perrault started hitting on me I had the sense to get away. I used to ride my bike about a mile and a half to church (Annunciation) to go to the five o'clock evening mass. I remember Perrault coming outside a lot and saying that he noticed me sitting in the church a lot and how he admired that in a young man. He wanted to know if I would serve mass for him. I told him, "No, not interested."

At the time he was in his forties. He was in the Air Force Reserve and talked about how he would someday make general. He'd see me sitting outside the church and he'd come out, usually in his black pants and shirt and white collar, and sometimes in his blue Air Force uniform—dark-blue pants and light-blue, short-sleeved shirt.

After my experiences with Smith, something told me to start staying away from priests, especially those who admired young men and who wanted them to serve their masses.

He always kept after me, though.

His method was the same as Smith's. He was over at our house a lot to ingratiate himself to my parents. He was always at Dad's cigar and tobacco shop, and I'd see him there. He'd often tell me what a great young man I was.

I was a senior in high school when my brother Jeff and I and another kid agreed to help Perrault move out of his place at the Landmark Apartments in Albuquerque's Uptown area. It was a crazy thing because the Landmark was basically Albuquerque's first high-rise luxury apartment building. He didn't live in the rectory. Not him. The talk was that he didn't get along with the other priests in the rectory and that he needed a place for himself. He apparently used his Air Force money to pay for it.

We got there—I don't remember what floor it was on, but it was pretty high up there. I was shocked. To me it looked like a love palace: big leather sofas and chairs, a big TV and a wooden, four-post bed with a canopy. I remember thinking, "What the hell? This guy's a priest. He took a vow of poverty. What the hell is he doing living in this nice place?"

We were there for three or four hours helping him move. At one point Perrault started pawing Jeff and me. He propositioned Jeff in his bedroom. He started grabbing my balls and said he wanted me to have sex with him on his bed because he wanted to do it one last time before he moved.

Don't know how he would have known to hit on me other than that Smith probably bragged to him about his exploits with me. I understand that child-raping priests often talked to each other about their prey and victims. Smith probably wanted to share me with Perrault.

Perrault grabbed me and insisted that we do it right then and there. As I said, I had had enough of God's representatives on earth by then, and I had only three words for Perrault before we three fled the place:

"Go fuck yourself."

****

One of your priests—sorry, man of God—used to take us high school boys and girls backpacking in the mountains. I was on two of those trips. Guess how your priest hiked? In the nude! In the nude with teenage boys and girls. He was another guy who talked a lot about sexuality and genitals.

I won't name him here because he wasn't named in my letter of intent to sue the Archdiocese of Santa Fe. But he is in my deposition. When he was phoned and asked if he had hiked naked with teens, he refused to answer. He refused three times to answer.

I'm not a prude by any means—got five kids—but that seems a lot fucked up to me.

How about you guys? Do you think that's wrong? Maybe this stuff just turns you guys on.

Does it?

"I have heard priests and Bishops explain, 'What more do they want?' Basically they want complete honesty, which includes a concerted effort to comprehend just how horrendous and toxic, not only the actual sexual abuse has been, but this ongoing official church response as well."— Fr. Thomas Doyle, November 30, 2007, affidavit.

Five

Soul Murder

Dear all of You, Friends, Relatives and Family Members:

So many times I've had to endure the pain of hearing people, who, when they talk about priest rape, don't have a clue as to what happened to me and what went through my mind and the minds of all those other kids who were raped.

I've heard the whispers behind my back—the whispers, the innuendo, the pity and the disgust—all from people who've never had the decency or guts to talk to me directly.

Their comments sicken me. "I would have kicked him in the balls," is one you hear from a lot of alleged tough guys. "I would have gone straight to my parents," is another. "Me and my buddies would have gone over and kicked their asses," is, of course, another.

Or how about this one: "Just get over it." That's what most others in the family have told me too many times: "Just get over it."

Do you have any idea how I'd like to get over this? Do you think I like living in this Hell with flashbacks and blackouts and puking fits and the anger and the rage and the shame and guilt and the feeling that I'm a worthless piece of human garbage and the feeling that I can't hang on and the feeling that at any second my head is going to explode and spew my vile, dirty brain all over the place? Do you think I like feeling that I need to crack open my skull and take my brain out and scrub it with a toilet brush?

Do you think I look forward to going to sleep and having a black, moaning, misty, claw-handed evil shroud chase me? If I could actually deny that all this happened to me, I would.

Just get over it? Tell me, how? How would you "just get over it" if you had been raped by a priest, if you had to watch a fat, evil pig masturbate all over a hotel room and then cum on you?

I would like nothing more than to "just get over it." Do any of you have the formula?

Tell me, how?

Let me put it to you this way: I'd like all of you who say "just get over it" to envision that your child or grandson or godchild is in a line with other kids outside a room—they're all beautiful children—and inside the room is an evil person who is going to strip your child or grandson or godchild and rape him. No, it's more than rape. That word isn't strong enough. Imagine that the fat, smelly, evil monster will strip himself, cackle, tear the clothes off your child in a mad, perverted frenzy, masturbate, spew his cum on that innocent thing, and then bend over and spread his fat, flabby, hairy, shit-encrusted ass cheeks and shout out to your child, "Fuck me, little boy! Fuck me up the ass. I love it up the ass."

And imagine that child—that confused, terrified, trembling thing—sobbing inside and knowing that he's trapped, that he can't scream for his parents, that his parents or aunts and uncles and brothers and sisters aren't there to protect him and kill the monster and carry him away to safety. And imagine your child silently and desperately praying to God for deliverance: "Oh dear God, most loving and holy one. Dear

God, protector of us children, deliver me from this evil, from this nightmare, from this hell on earth."

Imagine that confused and terrified child asking for God's help. Then imagine the monster saying to the kid, "Don't be afraid. Calm down, loosen up and get an erection—get that dick really hard for my asshole. And don't worry. God gave you these feelings. He gave them to me. He wants you to do this with me."

That's what happened to me.

Now, tell me, if that happened to you or to your child, would you "just get over it?" And, if that happened to your kid, would you go up to him and say, "just get over it?"

How do you "just get over it" knowing that the institution/business continues to shelter rapists and continues to treat us like shit? How do I "just get over it" when the institution refuses to admit its guilt and shame and refuses to ask for our forgiveness? How do I "just get over it" when all the cult offers us is half-hearted apologies, demands that we never question its authority and that we return to its "sacraments?"

What sacraments? Those people are frauds, liars and arrogant hypocrites—modern day Pharisees. That's what they are. A passage from the Catholic Encyclopedia describes what they've become:

> In many passages of the Gospels, Christ is quoted as warning the multitude against them in scathing terms. "The scribes and the Pharisees have sitten in the chair of Moses. All things therefore whatsoever they shall say to you, observe and do: but according to their works do ye not; for they say and do not. For they bind heavy and insupportable burdens, and lay them on men's shoulders; but with a finger of their own they will not move them. And all their works they do for to be seen of men."

"For they say and do not." That's these guys. It fits them perfectly. They say they're dealing appropriately with rapacious priests, but they refuse to give them up to civil authorities for prosecution.

So, all of you, how would you "just get over it?" I'm getting over it by writing this book.

Here's a clue for all of you: I don't want to hold onto this. I don't want to be identified by this. I don't want to be a victim. I wish to be free of this. That is my heart's desire.

No one seems to understand how and why it is that I and all the others kept silent and said nothing while this vile shit was occurring.

I've told you about the shame, guilt and sense of worthlessness and the sense that a man of God told me to do this. An authority figure. A religious authority figure. A religious authority figure whose authority I and my family believed in absolutely.

As I said before, I thought that priests were better than us, that they were closer to God than we were, that they had a connection to God that we didn't have, that no one—not even my parents—would believe the word of a fifteen-year-old over that of a man of God.

So I'll let the fine people of the Philadelphia grand jury that investigated Catholic priest rape from 2003 to 2005 tell you.

They interviewed more than a hundred witnesses, including victims, priests, bishops and the like and reported on more than a dozen cases. They issued their report on Sept. 15, 2005. It is horrifying, but truthful and enlightening reading:

A. The evidence reveals that child sexual abuse follows regular patterns.

When we gathered many of the Jurors did not understand the dynamics of clergy members' sexual abuse of minors. We could not understand how children who were so awfully abused could fail to tell anyone or, worse, would return to their abuser again and again. We learned from one of the leading American experts in the field, Kenneth Lanning, formerly of the Federal Bureau of Investigation, that the answer lies in the twisted relationship that acquaintance molesters initiate with their victims.

Those who prey on children first are careful in selecting their victims. They seek out vulnerable children who are needy for attention, often because of difficulties at home, because vulnerable children are easiest to mold to the abuser's desires. They then achieve power over their victims in a process that the experts call "grooming." Child molesters have enormous patience, identifying and pursuing victims sometimes for months before initiating the abuse. One might take a child to the beach, the cinema, the local ice cream parlor, showering his prey with toys and treats. He will give his victim what the child believes is benign attention and "love." Abusers also often befriend the families of their victims, visiting their homes, becoming dinner guests, exploiting parishioners' reverence for the priesthood. The parents are pleased and flattered by a priest's attentions to their children.

What surprised the Jurors most in Lanning's lengthy testimony was that so many of these men came across as "nice guys," that they can be so outwardly likeable. Mothers and fathers like them. The children who are their targets often love them. These are not "Stranger Danger" predators who look shady or menacing; they are the pillars of the Catholic community, respected and admired by all. Meanwhile, many of the targeted children do not understand sex in the first instance, so that when the priest reaches the point where he begins to act out sexually, the victims are utterly defenseless. As the abuse continues, their initial confusion turns to guilt and shame over what they believe they have allowed to happen. Many victims continue to think that priests can do no wrong or feel responsible for making a "good" priest go bad.

For the vulnerable child who craves love and security, and the devout child raised never to question the clergy's authority, it becomes nearly impossible to break free from the abusive priest, even after the sexual abuse begins. Experts refer to this phenomenon as the "trauma bond." Even though the abusive relationship is terribly damaging to the victim, he finds it difficult to remove himself from it because of the priest's power over him and the psychological and emotional bond that has resulted.

1. Sexually abused children rarely report their abuse.

Related to the question of why victims seem unable to break free of their abusers is the question of why it takes some victims decades to report priest sexual abuse. We learned there are many reasons for delayed reporting. Most of the victims are devout and/or come from devout families. Therefore, many of them regard priests as God's representatives on Earth. The well-educated priests, for their part, know very well the esteem in which trusting children and their parents hold them, and they manipulate that trust to ensure the victims' silence. Some of the priests whose cases we examined told their victims that God had sanctioned the sexual relationship and would punish them if they revealed it. Others told children that they loved them, and that the sexual abuse should be their little secret. Still others told their prey that they, the victims, were responsible for the abuse, and that no one would believe them if they told.

Psychological denial is not an unusual response to trauma, confusion, shame and despair. And there are other, powerful disincentives to report a priest's abuse. Some victims fear damaging the Church's reputation. Others fear their parents' disbelief or anger—not toward the priest, but toward them. Some worry that such a horrific revelation could destroy their parents' sustaining faith in the Church. Many adolescent boys fear that revealing sexual contact with a man could call into question whether they are heterosexual.

2. The lifelong impact extends from isolation to "soul murder."

The priests' manipulation of their victims, we found, can be as cunning as it is cruel. Often the offenders isolate their victims from others, dominating their time, criticizing their parents and friends, and discouraging activities outside of the church and the priest's presence. The victims come to believe that the abusive relationship is the only one they have. This strategy of isolating victims not only deprives them of someone in whom they might confide; it also serves the priest's purpose—to continue the abusive relationship. Subsequently, the isolation becomes one of the cruelest consequences of abuse, destroying families and lasting decades.

We saw victims who had been told by their abuser that their parents had sanctioned the priest's actions. In two cases, the victims discovered only recently, as they prepared to testify before the Grand Jury, that what the priest had told them was not true. For 20 years they had been estranged from their parents, sometimes hating them, because they believed that their parents had knowingly allowed their abuse. If a priest and God could betray them, how could they know that their parents had not as well? Parents, for their part, cannot understand their abused children, who for no apparent reason have turned their backs on school, church, friends and family. Who suddenly are not fun-loving and happy, but sullen and withdrawn. Who are abusing alcohol and drugs and acting out in other ways. The parents blame their children.

Meanwhile, if other children suspect a boy is being abused, they often ridicule the victim, suggesting he is homosexual. And not just children do this. We heard testimony about a nun, the teacher of one victim, who—after the boy reported his abuse to police— began calling him by a girl's name in class, eliciting giggles from his fellow students.

Most devastating of all, we saw firsthand what Father Thomas Doyle calls "soul murder." As Father Doyle, a conscientious Dominican priest who has assisted clergy abuse victims around the world points out, these children suffer from the abuse not just physically and psychologically, but spiritually. The faith they need to cope with the tragedies of life is for them forever defiled. In order for a priest to satisfy his sexual impulses, these children lose their innocence, their virginity, their security, and their faith. It is hard to think of a crime more heinous.

3. Priests who abuse minors have many victims.

Another thing we learned about sexual abuse of minors is that the offenders typically have numerous victims. We heard from experts that the compulsion that drives some priests to molest or rape children is not curable, that treatment and supervision need to be intense and lifelong, and that the recidivism rate is extremely high. In the files of Philadelphia Archdiocese priests that we obtained by subpoena, we saw what must have been crystal-clear as well to Cardinals Krol and Bevilacqua and their aides: that many, many priests each have had many, many victims, often spanning decades.

The experts told us that, given the nature of the crime, victims who report their abuse represent merely the tip of the iceberg, and that abusive priests likely have preyed on many more victims who have not come forward. We heard reports, most of which the Archdiocese had also received, about 16 victims of Fr. Nicholas Cudemo, 14 victims of Fr. Raymond Leneweaver, 17 victims of Fr. James Brzyski, and 18 victims of Fr. Albert Kostelnick. We believe there were many more.

It is hard to think of a crime more heinous, or more deserving of strict penalties and an unlimited statute of limitations, than the sexual abuse of children. This is especially so when the perpetrators are priests—men who exploit the clergy's authority and access to minors, as well as the trust of faithful families, to prey on children in order to gratify perverted urges. After reviewing thousands of documents from Archdiocese files and hearing statements and testimony from over a hundred witnesses—including Archdiocese managers, priests, abuse victims and experts on the Church and child abuse—we, the Grand Jurors, were taken aback by the extent of sexual exploitation within the Philadelphia Archdiocese. We were saddened to discover the magnitude of the calamity in terms of the abuse itself, the suffering it caused, and the numbers of victims and priests involved.

The Jurors heard testimony that will stay with us for a very long time, probably forever. We heard of Philadelphia-area priests committing countless acts of sexual depravity against children entrusted to their care through the Archdiocese's parishes and schools. The abuses ranged from glancing touches of genitals under the guise of innocent wrestling to sadomasochistic rituals and relentless anal, oral and vaginal rapes. We found that no matter what physical form the abuse took, or how often it was repeated, the damage to these children's psyches was devastating. Not only were the victims betrayed by a loved and revered father figure, but they also faced lifelong guilt and shame, isolation from family and peers, and torments that typically included alcoholism, addictions, martial difficulties, and sometimes thoughts of suicide. In many cases, we discovered, the victims believed God had abandoned them.

For any who might want to believe that the abuse problem in the Philadelphia area was limited in scope, this Report will disabuse them of that impression. The Jurors heard from some victims who were sexually abused once or twice, and from many more who were abused week after week for years. Many of the priests whose cases we examined had more than 10 victims; some abused multiple victims simultaneously. Indeed, the evidence arising from the Philadelphia Archdiocese reveals criminality against minors on a widespread scale—sparing no geographic sector, no income level, no ethnic group. We heard testimony about priests molesting and raping children in rectory bedrooms, in church sacristies, in parked cars, in swimming pools, at Saint Charles Borromeo Seminary, at the priests' vacation homes in the Poconos and the Jersey Shore, in the children's schools and even in their homes.

From all the documents and testimony put before us, we have received a tragic education—about the nature of child abuse, for example: how predators manipulate their prey, why the abuse so often goes unreported, how its impact on the victims and their families remains lifelong. Even so, we find it hard to comprehend or absorb the full extent of the malevolence and suffering visited on this community, under cover of clerical collar, by powerful, respected and rapacious priests.

****

As I got older and in my junior and senior years in high school, I got stronger physically and emotionally and was able to break away from Smith, although not totally. His diabetes was becoming severe and he was being shipped off to the Paracletes in Jemez Springs. He'd call, though, always to talk about the joys of masturbation and to try to get me to go on another trip with him. He continued to call even after I had started college here in Albuquerque.

There were a few times when he was in town that we went to a Pizza Hut on Lomas Boulevard and we'd sit and talk about the priesthood and he'd drink enormous amounts of beer. Yeah, even then I was still considering the priesthood.

I was free of the atrocity of the physical abuse and the rapes, but I wasn't free of the emotional pain and torment. There are a couple of other stories to this twisted, sick relationship that I'll get to later.

To this day they make me puke my guts out.

"I'm a filthy, dirty human being. I contend that I live in a prison of shame. I don't believe there's a place for me in this world."—Larry Monte Jr. deposition, April 23, 2007.

Six

Thirty-eight Years of a Living Hell—the Effects of Being Raped by a Priest

Dear Pigs:

I'd rather do anything than write what I'm about to. But I have to write it because you people and everyone else in this world, especially all you Catholics, need to know what being raped by a priest does to a person. It does murder your soul. I can't think of anything more painful and sorrowful—so absolutely dehumanizing—than what I'm about to say. It comes straight from my deposition when I filed a claim against your bureaucracy:

A. I don't know how I've had five children. I mean, having sexual relationships with my wife is just—I mean, I have nightmares. I can't do it. I go into a hotel room, I freak out. I won't bathe in a hotel because of what he did with them. I don't sleep. I wake up in cold sweats. I have nightmares constantly. I'm never at peace. I don't enjoy life.

Q. How long has this been going on?

A. Since I was 16 years old. And it's only getting worse.

Q. And you associate those with the sexual abuse by the priests?

A. I just thought being miserable was a part of life.

Q. When did you begin to associate what you've just described for me as being caused by the sexual abuse by the priests?

A. When I got married.

Q. What was it about you getting married that you associated these problems with having been sexually abused?

A. Having sexual relationships with my wife was just incredibly painful.

Q. Psychologically painful or physically painful?

A. Physically, too.

Q. In what way is it physically painful?

A. I couldn't perform. Couldn't do it. It was real embarrassing. I was ashamed. I mean, I could sometimes.

Q. Okay.

A. I had five kids.

Q. But when you would be having—trying to have sexual contact with your wife, you associated all these problems you had because you were abused?

A. All I could see—visualize his fat ass on my face. That's all I'd see.

Q. And that's been true for a long time?

A. Since I was—yeah, since I've been married.

Jean and I were married in 1980. And all these thirty years when I've tried to make love to my beautiful, my wonderful, my incredible, my loving wife, the woman who has been with me through all of this, the woman I love and who loves me, the woman who should have left me long ago but didn't, all I've been able to see is Robert John Smith's fat, sweaty, hairy, flabby, smelly, slimy, shit-speckled, hemorrhoidal ass in my face.

How's that for abuse? How's that for being in a living hell and being a walking dead man for thirty-eight years? How's that for misery? How's that for pure, unmitigated horror? How's that for sexual dysfunction? That's what this is about, seeing a shit-speckled, hemorrhoidal ass in my face when I try to make love to my wife.

Your priest and your organization did that to me.

You and Smith did it to me back then—you failed to protect me and all of us from your raping priests—you did it to me in that deposition, and you continue to do it to me today as you continue to harbor rapists and refuse to sufficiently acknowledge our pain, suffering, horror and humiliation.

I had to sit for four or five hours through that deposition, and every second of it was hell. I felt slimy, filthy and humiliated afterward.

I had to sit in a room with lawyers and a court reporter and talk about this stuff. Your lawyer spent god knows how much time asking me what and how many jobs I'd had. He asked me about my brothers and sisters—as if that had anything to do with this. He was just trying to find some chink in my armor so you could deny my claim. That's what it was about. You and your lawyer were trying trip me up—to make me sound like an idiot and a fuckup just so you wouldn't have to dip into your vast finances and give some cash to a guy who was raped by your priest, who had his balls grabbed and squished, and who was nearly drowned by one and who sees a priest's ass in his face when he tries to make love to his wife.

The line of questioning was sickening. Your lawyer wanted to know about my sex life and too much more. I felt like I was talking to a sick and twisted voyeur who was getting his nuts off listening to how I was raped by a priest. He was dark and cold-hearted and could have cared less for the redemption of my soul. He wasn't about loving, forgiveness and helping me heal; he was just there to rip open my soul. And that's what he did; ripped it open—ripped me open and gleefully threw a ton of salt on my raw, bleeding, oozing wounds.

His twisted and sickening line of questioning was as perverse as what Smith did to me. It added new and more torture to an already tortured past. I can't help but wonder if all you club members get a twisted sense of joy out of reading these depositions. Why couldn't we have just met on the basis of helping one another as Christ would have wanted?

You see, I never wanted to sue you and your corporation. I didn't want money. I wanted only a few things from you people: A full acknowledgment of my pain, humiliation and suffering, a heart-felt apology and vow to reform and turn the rapists over to the law, a cleansing of your house, and a humble request for my forgiveness. I was hoping for Christ-like behavior on your part. Instead, you tortured and humiliated me again. You people don't practice what you preach. Will you ever?

The apology never came. Instead I got letters and phone calls about how these rapes happened forty years ago, how they didn't happen under Sheehan's watch, how I should return to the club that raped me and how you're going to continue to protect your child-raping criminals.

Is there any more egregious and evil act than knowingly and willingly destroying the innocence of your greatest resource, a child? Your arrogance and wanton disregard for all of us has destroyed, in my mind, any and all good you have done.

You cared only about legalities, not about me or my healing. You put a price on my suffering and hoped I would just go away. That deposition was dehumanizing.

Are you beginning to get an idea—even just a little, just a tiny one, just a damn smidgen of one!—as to why I and so many others who've been raped by your priests hate you?

Do you understand why I tremble, sweat, get dizzy and puke when I drive by some of your churches—I mean buildings—and why I will never again walk into one of your structures?

Do you understand why, when you come out with new pronouncements on priest rape, as you did in July, 2010, and when you make no requirement that bishops turn the rapists over to the law, why I and others fly into a rage and want to beat down the walls of your evil empire and destroy it forever?

You need to be destroyed. You deserve it.

I'll bet you'd understand if you saw a fat, shit-speckled man's ass in your face every time you tried to make love to your wife. And I'll bet if you were us you'd be just as hateful and you'd react with shock, horror and disgust if one of your bureaucrats told you to pray about this and return to the sacraments of the one true church.

I think you'd react that way. Then again, maybe not. Maybe you guys would enjoy the scene.

Put yourselves in our minds. Come with me on a journey through my memories of what your cult, bureaucracy and business knowingly and willingly gave me.

You won't because you don't want to acknowledge that your people abused authority in the sickest, most inhumane and evil way possible; that they and you committed heretical blasphemy in its purest form.

Do all you people who continue to sit in those pews and give these people money—people who refuse to turn child rapists over to law enforcement authorities—understand why I think you're aiding and abetting crimes and criminals?

I'll bet you would if you or one of your kids was raped by a priest.

And let's make this clear: It's not sexual abuse. It's rape! It's child rape!

If you or your kid was raped would you want the perpetrator handed over to the cops? Or, would you want a secretive club to shelter the monster because he's special?

What would you want?

Do you people know why I think you're mindless, thoughtless sheep? Do you even think about this? Think!

You Church bureaucrats just refused to make it mandatory for bishops to turn over child rapists to the law. You'll kick a guy out of the priesthood for being a homosexual, but you'll protect child rapists and work with them.

If that's not twisted and sick, I don't know what is.

A Fateful Phone Call

It was Oct. 13, 2006, when the phone rang in my cigar shop on Louisiana Boulevard just north of Menaul in Albuquerque. It was around ten-thirty in the morning. The shop had been in the little strip mall since the mid-1970s when Dad got tired of the corporate world and bought it.

I got tired of the insurance business and bought it from him in 2004. It was small, but nice, and we had a small walk-in humidor. We've moved into a much larger place since then, and business is good.

Actually, I'll get to that phone call in a bit, but first, a little background.

I had, in the years since high school and Smith, tried to put this stuff out of my mind. At the time it seemed like I had done it, but in retrospect, I hadn't. Ask Jean. She'll tell you of the ruined days, my rages, my throwing furniture, my sweeping plates and silverware off tables with my arms, my sleepless nights when the shroud came, my anger, my bitterness, my shame, my guilt, my boozing, my recklessness, my feelings of utter worthlessness, my attempts to take neckties and pull them tighter and tighter and tighter around my neck, my attempts to put my head in a door frame and slam the door shut, and my trying to eat a gun.

I had vowed that no one would ever know about this—not even Jean—and that I'd take this filthy secret to my grave.

As I told the lawyers in my deposition, I was too ashamed to tell anyone. I thought I would be less than a man and less than a human being if anyone found out.

When I was going through it with Smith part of me knew it was wrong because I'd go home and scrub myself with a toilet brush afterwards.

I hated every minute of it, of course, but when you're exploring your sexuality with a man of God, well, I thought that I was probably gay. That's when I really started having problems. I didn't know whether I was gay, and I didn't know whether I was straight. I just didn't know. My head was swimming .

I didn't tell anyone at the time because I was so ashamed and guilty and feeling worthless. I felt like I had somehow caused Smith to do those things to me, that I was the perpetrator. That's how this shit makes you feel, like you're less than a man and less than human.

I'll back up to the early 1990s, which is when all this started busting loose on me. That's when attorney Bruce Pasternack and other lawyers in Albuquerque started filing the sexual abuse lawsuits against the Archdiocese of Santa Fe.

I was in Austin, Texas, working for Prevailing Fringe Benefits, which was my company, when I got a call from an attorney asking if I had known Smith and if I had been raped by him. I denied knowing anything about that stuff. As I said, no one was ever going to know.

But, the mind has its own plans. I started thinking and thinking about this stuff and I got angrier and angrier and started drinking more. It was somewhere in Texas that I once tried to strangle myself with a tie. I was standing in front of Jean and I yanked it tighter and tighter and tighter around my neck. She was horrified and screamed at me to stop.

Then one day in 1994 my phone rang. I'll never forget it. It was Mom with a concerned voice.

She was in tears because Robert Smith had been named in one of the Albuquerque newspapers. He and the archdiocese had been sued, and he had been named as a child molester and rapist. She asked me, "Did anything ever happen to you?"

"No, Mom. Don't worry about it," I told her.

Jeff was my chief financial officer at the time. I told him about Mom's call and he asked if anything had ever happened to me. I told him nothing had.

I started getting worse and worse. There was more anger and rage and booze. Jean was wondering what was wrong. One day she asked, and I told her that I had been sexually abused by a priest. I didn't give her any details. That was in 1995.

We had been married for fifteen years by then, and for those fifteen years I had lied to my wife. That's how vile this stuff is. For fifteen years I lied to my wife! I kept Smith's and your sick organization's secret, which is exactly what you people wanted.

Can you imagine being Jean and finding that out? Can you imagine the betrayal she must have felt at not being told for fifteen years? Do you see what I did? I became one of your accomplices.

It was starting to eat at me, so at one point I picked up the phone and called Sister Nancy Kazik, who was the archdiocese's child abuse liaison. I had gotten the Albuquerque papers and seen her name in an article.

I talked to Kazik and told her what had happened. I said I was one of the abused kids, that I wasn't going to bring a lawsuit and that I just wanted them to be aware of it. I guess at the time all I wanted was an apology. I never got it.

Then, in 1994, when I was back in Albuquerque, I got a call from Archbishop Michael Sheehan. He infuriated me then, and he continues to infuriate me.

Sheehan told me that none of the abuse had happened under his watch, that it happened a long time ago and that he was cleaning it up. He assured me that it would never happen again. Then he went on and on and talked about my father and my family and how he liked cigars and, you know, what he liked to smoke. He said he would pray for me. I remember that he would pray for me. That much came out, "You're in our prayers." I remember hanging up the phone and wondering what the hell that was all about?

That's when it really began hitting me that Sheehan and everyone else in your sick club won't take responsibility for the abuse, turn the rapists over to civil authorities, defrock them, clean house, apologize to me and everyone else and ask for our forgiveness.

If you only know how many times I have offered you people forgiveness, only to be insulted by you.

I was still going to church, believe it or not. Our kids were in Catholic school. But each and every day I was losing more and more control. I started reading scriptures, as I had done in grade school and in high school. I started reading Church teachings, and I slowly started coming to the conclusion that the Catholic Church is about hypocrisy, control and lies. Most of your rules don't have anything to do about what's actually in scripture. You just want to control people.

In Austin I had started seeing a shrink for this. Her name was Mary Tonsager. I had never seen a shrink before other than the time I went to one as a cop after I had shot and killed a drug dealer in Beaumont, Texas. I was a cop for three years from 1981 to 1983.

I saw Mary six or seven times. That stuff wasn't for me. You know, you're a guy and you think that shrink stuff is for wusses. Mary sent me to another shrink who put me on Zoloft and some other medications for anxiety. It helped.

But all through these years the black, evil shroud kept coming, and it kept coming more and more frequently. I couldn't sleep. I could barely think straight when I was awake. I was filled with this unending rage, shame, guilt and feeling of worthlessness. I felt like a piece of human shit.

Then, in 2002, it really started breaking loose. The priest sex abuse scandals started breaking in Boston and the east coast. I read and watched as bishops and cardinals tried to dismiss it as the fault of the news media. I was disgusted and enraged that you people wouldn't take responsibility for your child rapists.

At one point I wrote Sheehan to ask him why the Church—I was actually still a believer, but becoming less so—wasn't firing all of the child rapist priests and that I was thinking of quitting the club. The letter I got back from him severed my ties with your club/gang/bureaucracy forever. Here's what he wrote in his July 19, 2002, letter:

"Most of the sexual abuse of minors by priests happened 20, 30, or 40 years ago and many of the priests are deceased. You expressed concern that all of the guilty priests have not been laicized or defrocked, but it may be that you don't understand the distinction between restriction and laicization.

"Church teaching is that 'Thou are a priest forever according to the order of Melchizedek.' It is very difficult in the universal law of the Catholic Church for forced laicization to take place since ordination is forever. However, to restrict [a] priest and allow him no further ministry whatsoever is the action that was taken.

"It is a grave a[nd] heavy punishment for the priest and it also protects children from further contact with that priest.

"I think it is important, Larry, to look for the truth of the Catholic faith and to not leave it because of human weakness and the evil that was done 20, 30 or 40 years ago. The Church has the fullness of the teachings of Jesus and in no other Church will you find the Mass with the Body and Blood of Christ. In no other religion will you find the unbroken line of the apostolic succession going all the way back to the Apostles."

To say I was enraged is, well, understatement is too mild a word. I have never gotten a more arrogant, clueless, condescending piece of crap than that letter. To me it says, "You poor, stupid fool. Do you not know who we are? We're from the order of Melchizedek. We're better than you. We're a gang unto ourselves. We're above the law. Stay with us who have fucked you and let us give you the sacraments. You're just a piece of shit who must obey us."

The order of Melchizedek? Fuck you!

Jesus kicked money changers out of the temple, and you can't kick child rapists out of your club? You know what that tells me? That you're above any of our laws. That you're a law unto yourselves. Is not your behavior similar to the way the Pharisees would rebut things? Is that the meaning of Christ?

Eight years later I'm still disgusted. There was no apology, no saying, "Hey, we screwed up and we were wrong and we hurt you and *will you forgive us?* We're turning these rapists over to civil authorities and will aggressively seek and assist in their prosecution. Our organization has no place for child rapists. We know we hurt you and we will do everything we can to help you heal and get well."

And what is this stuff about being a priest forever? Is this the Mob? Maybe you're the original and only true Mob.

You'll defrock priests for being gay and for screwing around with women, and, who knows, maybe even if their chalices aren't of the precise metallic composition that your goofy rules require, but you can't get rid of child-raping priests?

I might be dumb, but I'm not stupid. You guys are frauds and liars. You are not the church that Jesus had in mind when he said, "Peter, upon this rock build my church."

I don't recall anywhere in scripture where Jesus said, "Peter, build a church that controls people with insane rules, demands their money—even conjures up the idea of Purgatory to get it—and protects men who rape little boys and girls. Oh, and by the way, Pete, don't ever apologize to, or ask for the forgiveness of those whose lives your ordained rapists will destroy. Just make it sound like they're the losers, fuckups, sinners and idiots and tell them *they need to forgive you* and return to the club. Use every psychological ploy necessary to control them. In short, just fuck them."

Can't find it anywhere. You people obviously have, because that's how you operate.

****

It was while I was in Austin that I had another fun—how about memorable—experience at your gang's behest. I was growing more confused and anxious by the day. Part of me wanted to kill myself. The other part, who knows, all I know is that every moment now seemed to be Hell here on earth. I was trembling, puking, raging, seeing that shroud at night, boozing and trying everything I could to hang on to some sense of sanity and dignity. It was like I was in a forty-foot-deep hole that was getting deeper, and because its walls were slimy mud, every time I tried to climb out I just slipped and slid and fell back down. It's as if I was desperately gouging my fingernails into those mud walls in an attempt to get even the slightest hold in an effort to get just a little off the ground.

I made the biggest mistake of my life, though, and I hope no one else who has ever been raped by a priest makes it. I turned to the bureaucracy for help.

You can see by Sheehan's letter what a mistake that was. Why would I—would anyone—return to the bureaucracy for redemption? They're the ones who perpetrated the crime. I don't like using this term, but I have to now. The club is nothing but a cult. You guys suck people in, get them to feel guilty about everything, refuse to fire rapists and then tell me that I'm supposed to go to you for redemption.

I'd been talking with people, and someone—can't remember who—suggested that I undergo an exorcism. I agreed, and it was one of the worst things I've ever done.

I went to a priest's office in Austin. It was a small place with a large crucifix on one wall and a certificate of something or other on another.

The exorcising priest and I talked for a while, and he asked me what was going on. I told him about the shroud and how my heart was bleeding, and bleeding faster every day. I don't remember much other than that he said some prayers during the two-and-a-half hours I was in his office. I don't know if he splashed me with holy water. I think that if he had it would have steamed up. That's how I felt. I felt like I was the evil one.

I left that office more confused. It started hitting me. What the fuck did I do wrong? Why had I needed an exorcism? Smith and the bureaucracy are the ones who screwed me.

Somehow I managed to hang on through the ensuing years. It wasn't pretty. I hated sleeping and I hated being awake. I hated being sober. I hated being me. More and more the feeling of shame and guilt and worthlessness and unworthiness were consuming me. I felt that there was no place for me in this world.

It was in September of 2006 that everything fell apart for good. I remember fastening a few belts together in the upstairs bedroom of our home, hitching one end to the door knob, throwing the other over the door, making a loop with that end and then testing it with my arms and full weight to make sure the door would hold so I could hang myself. Jean caught me before I could slip the loop around my neck and lift my legs off the floor.

Another time Jean caught me with my head between a door and its frame as I was getting ready to slam the door on my head. How I wanted that door to smash my skull and crack it open. How I wanted my filthy, unworthy brain to spill out onto the floor.

One time I picked up a chair in our living room, lifted it over my head and slammed it down on the coffee table. It took a big chunk out of that table. One of those nights, I think it was the attempted hanging, Jean had the sense to call our friend, Sgt. Pat Apodaca of the Albuquerque Police Department. He drove over in his squad car. He approached me as I slumped in a chair in the bedroom and talked me down. He also said he was going to drive me to a hospital, and that because I was a danger to myself, police protocol required that I be handcuffed. I couldn't bear the shame of being cuffed. I couldn't believe that I was that fucked up.

But I was.

Pat is an incredible cop, human being and friend. He was kind that evening and said he wouldn't cuff me. He let me ride in the front seat for the seven-mile ride to Presbyterian Kaseman Hospital in Albuquerque.

There I talked to a shrink who gave me some anti-depressants. They kept me overnight. The next morning Jean came to pick me up. I wasn't there. I was so disgusted and angry and full of shame and guilt that I decided to leave and walk the seven miles home. Somehow, Jean found me. She shouted from her rolled down car window for me to get into the car. I refused. She kept following as I walked and she kept pleading with me to get in. I refused each plea. Finally she drove away and I continued the walk home.

All I can say is that right then I wanted to be dead.

****

Now to that fateful phone call.

It was October 13, 2006. I had bought the cigar shop from Dad two years earlier and was running it. We've got thousands of customers and it's a good and fun business. But that day, it wasn't.

Dad was still alive, and he and others in the family had written Sheehan to ask him to help get me psychological help. They had seen how I was deteriorating and drinking and trying to kill myself. They had implored me to get help. I had seen a couple of other shrinks in those years, but I never kept it up. It was about ten-thirty in the morning when phone rang in the office behind the checkout counter. I picked it up. It was Sheehan calling, apparently for Dad. He didn't know it was me on the line. His sickening voice repeated the things he had written in that 2002 letter: That all this happened thirty and forty years ago, that he had cleaned things up, and that Larry needed to return to the Church and its sacraments.

I dropped the phone and walked out the back door and went walking down the alley behind the half-block-long strip mall. I can't even say that my head was spinning. It—every piece of me—was in the most excruciating pain I had ever been in. I really couldn't see anything. Everything was a blur. I was stumbling around. I wanted to cry but I couldn't. Oh the pain, the pain, the pain, the pain! I couldn't take it anymore. Not a second more of it.

I stumbled and stumbled and stumbled, and, well, I'll let Jean pick up the story:

I had gotten to work that morning and Larry's sister Katie was in the shop and she came running outside and asked frantically, "Have you seen Larry? Something has happened to him. He got a phone call. I think it was from the archbishop. I think he talked to Larry."

We went in the store and looked around. Larry wasn't there. Then we went a few stores down where we had our cigar club and looked for him there. He wasn't there either.

We searched all over and Katie went back to the alley behind the shop. She walked down a few stores and she found Larry beside a dumpster sitting on steps that led to a metal door to one of the stores. He was burning his arms and hands with a cigar and banging his head into the door. He was burning himself with a cigar! I have no idea how we got him up or how we got him again to Kaseman, but we did.

Do you know what it's like to see your husband burn himself and bang his head into a metal door? Does anyone know what that's like? I wanted to cry and scream, but I couldn't because I had to do something. I had to save my husband's life.

****

That was a Friday morning. They got me to the hospital and I saw a couple of shrinks and told them that I had been raped by your priest. They laced me into a straitjacket and diagnosed me with Posttraumatic Stress Disorder, kept me there and said I needed extended treatment.

That Tuesday they released me to my brother Dan who flew with me to Wickenburg, Arizona, and a thirty-day stay at The Meadows, a long-term, inpatient treatment center.

You know why I burned myself? Because physical pain is easier to take than the mental anguish you have caused me for thirty-eight years. Because when I mutilate myself it takes my mind off the thought that I was fucked in the ass and cummed on by your priest. It takes my mind off Fr. Robert John Smith giving me blow jobs and demanding them in return. It frees me temporarily from the memory of that fat, smelly pig whacking off and cumming into a glass to measure his load. It frees me from the porn, the booze, the pills, the talk of the joy of masturbation and the talk that God wanted me to fuck your priest. It frees me from the memory of the Red Raider Inn and those motel rooms in Clovis and Socorro and Carlsbad and Santa Fe and Lubbock and Pecos. It frees me from the memory of having your priest start out trips where he knew he was going to fuck me by saying the rosary. I'd rather be burned at the stake than go through those motel rooms again. Sometimes I wished I had been.

Do you know why I was banging my head into that door? Because I wanted to crack my skull open, take out my brain and wash it and scrub it and cleanse it of the filth that your priest put into it. Scrub it with lye and a toilet brush of all those sick, vile memories. Scrub it of the idea that I brought the rapes on myself, that I was the perpetrator, that I had been less than holy, that I had caused a man of God to rape a teenager. Scrub it of the thoughts that I was a dirty, worthless and unworthy piece of shit. Scrub it of the idea that I was rotten to the core. Scrub it of my shame. Scrub it of all memories of you people and your sick and twisted club.

"I thought it was me. I'm doing something wrong. Oh my gosh, I'm not doing this wife thing right. I'm not keeping the house clean. I'm not cooking the right things. I'm not keeping the kids clean."—Jean Monte

Seven

The Circle of Destruction

Dear Protectors of Child Rapists:

The evil of what your priests and you have done is that you've ruined more than one life. Sexual abuse forms its own ever-expanding web and circle of victims and screwed up lives. If it were just my life that went to hell I might be able to live with it. But Smith and you people got more than just me. You got my wife, my kids, my mother, my father, my brothers and my sisters and plenty of others I've dealt with over these past thirty-eight years. And I hate you for it.

I'm going to stop here for a while and let Jean tell you about it. Maybe since she wasn't raped by your priest you'll understand. So here's Jean:

I know that a lot of people are tired of hearing about this subject and wish it would go away, but you all need to understand that it doesn't go away. Larry lives with it every day of his life. I live with it. Our kids live with it. It is our "normal."

The Church has made some half-hearted apologies, but they won't mean anything to us until all these guys are in jail.

That's what I'm having trouble wrapping my head around. These were criminal acts. Why haven't the police been called?

It seems like the people who run the Church are from a different generation, one where children were treated as property and their feelings didn't matter. Children weren't considered people until they got to a certain age. They were forced to work at an early age and they were beaten and abused and they were just supposed to outgrow it and let it go.

It's like, "Okay, you're an adult now, move on and get over it, let it go."

It seems that the heads of the Church are so old that they don't understand the physical, emotional and spiritual damage this has done, and so they minimize everything. Well, the abuse will continue to happen until there is a new generation of Church leaders that recognizes the value of children and become proponents of the value of children.

For a church that is so right-to-life and says that a child in the womb is sacred, but then says that once it is born you can do anything you want with it, well, that's wrong. That's what I'm seeing.

Throughout our first fifteen years of marriage I thought I was the problem. Larry would rage and drink and withdraw and swear and hurt himself. We were both twenty-two when we married on Jan. 11, 1980, and who knows, I might have attributed it to our young ages. But as time wore on, I couldn't help but think that I was the problem, that I wasn't a good enough wife or friend or mother.

I thought that it was my fault, always—always my fault—and that if I just did more Larry wouldn't get so mad. It was that whole co-dependency spiral.

Larry would always make comments like, "If you really knew me you wouldn't stay with me." I'd ask what he meant, and he'd never say. He'd just sulk off and withdraw or rage. I couldn't figure it out.

It was in the early 1990s, fifteen years into our marriage, that he finally told me. He had gotten calls from the lawyers in Albuquerque asking him if he was one of those kids who were raped. I know now that he lied. It was after his mother called after seeing Smith's name in the Albuquerque papers that Larry told me. He said that Smith was one of the priests who had been accused.

I told him that it didn't surprise me. Then Larry said, "I've got to tell you now because I was hiding that from you and now you know. Please don't tell anyone. The kids can't ever know."

I didn't tell the kids. When Larry's mom called me to ask about Smith and Larry I basically lied to her. I kept it a secret until things really started falling apart in 2006. That's when we started telling the kids and the rest of the family.

Do you see what happened? Larry kept Smith's and your vile secret. He covered up for your crimes and your sins. And by agreeing to never tell anyone and lying about it, I became your secret keeper and accomplice in crime as well.

Larry's shame and guilt came to me.

Do you understand? Can you? I thought that I had caused his rages. I thought I was defective as a wife and mother. I thought that, like Larry, I too was unworthy. That's how evil this is. And it isn't just me. The kids have been affected too.

Our youngest son told me a while ago, "Mom, you know, we're messed up." Our oldest is just stonewalling it, and one of our other boys is angry. He's been holding it in like Larry has and he's been trying take care of Larry. He asked me recently, "Why won't he do something? Why won't he do something?"

My answer was that Larry is finally doing something. He's writing this book, and since April, 2010, he's been seeing Dr. Reinhart Schelert, D.Min., a man who has been treating sexual abuse victims for twenty years. It's been good, and Larry is starting to heal.

But it wasn't always that way. Even after we found Larry in the alley burning himself and banging his head into that door, and even after his thirty-day stay at The Meadows in Arizona, he was still reluctant to admit that he had a problem.

What a problem he has had.

We were living in Dallas and we were at home and Larry had tied his tie real tight and he told me that he couldn't get it off, and then I saw that he was just pulling it tighter and tighter around his neck and he was doing it on purpose. By that time he had told me about the rapes. All I could say to him was, "If you don't get help with this we are going to wind up scraping you off the floor. You need to get help now."

His answer was, "There is nobody who can help me with this."

I've taken a gun away from him. I've stopped him from sticking his head in a door frame and slamming the door shut on his head. I've seen him pick up a chair and slam it into our coffee table. I've seen him banging his head into the wall of our house outside our second-floor bedroom. He's swept dishes off tables and onto the floor and raged and raged. One year at Christmastime he was trying to put a fresh-cut Christmas tree in a stand. The kids were all around in the frontroom. Larry couldn't get it to stand straight in the stand and so he just blew up and said, "This is just stupid. Your dad can't do anything right."

It was a big tree. The whole thing fell over and Larry sulked off and went upstairs to the bedroom. We put the tree up.

I remember coming back to Austin one time from visiting my parents in Beaumont. Larry had stayed home. As I turned into the driveway I got a horrible feeling of dread because Larry's car was in the driveway. I wondered what he was doing home because it was mid-afternoon, and I thought to myself, "My God, he's done something." I figured I'd go in and see him hanging or something. I didn't want the kids to see so I told them that they had to stay in the car because we might have to go to the grocery store. I told them I'd have to go and check something real quick in the house. I ran in to make sure that Larry was alive. As I opened the door I had this feeling of total panic.

For the first fifteen years I didn't know what was troubling him, and I never knew when he would fly into a rage or withdraw. As I said before, I always thought it was my fault.

Larry had promised me that he wouldn't commit suicide—purposely, at least. He had told me that he had seen what suicide does to families and kids. He said he wouldn't do it. What he has done, though, is not take care of himself to the point where it has threatened his health. He's always said that I'd be better off without him.

There was one time in 1997 when we were in Austin when one of our sons had flown to Albuquerque to visit his grandparents. He was in seventh grade, and so when he came back, I made sure he had a direct flight from Albuquerque to Austin. I didn't want him to change flights when his plane stopped in Dallas. He was supposed to stay on the plane. Larry's mom had been out to visit us and when she was flying back to Albuquerque she had had to change planes in Dallas. So she told our son to change planes in Dallas, and he got off his plane in Dallas.

Well, Larry had gone to pick him up at the Austin airport and he never came off the plane because he had gotten off in Dallas like Larry's mom had told him. Oh my gosh, Larry went nuts. He called his mom and accused her of losing our son. He was in a rage. I had never seen him like that.

Larry's mom called and said it was an honest mistake. She asked me why Larry reacted the way he did. I said he was hypersensitive about the safety of his kids. She asked why. I didn't answer. She said, "Jean, you need to tell me what's going on."

I told her, "Peg, he asked me to never say anything." She said:

"He's one of those abused kids, isn't he?"

She said she had known the moment she had seen Smith's name in the newspapers.

"He was one of them, wasn't he?" she asked. I said:

"Peg, he asked me not to tell anybody." She just burst into tears over the telephone.

At that point I knew that his parents knew and so I had to tell Larry. I told him, "Your mom knows."

His response broke my heart.

"Was she mad at me?" he asked.

Larry can turn into a little kid. His face gets puffy and his eyes widen and he gets a hurt look on his face. He reverts back to being a fifteen year old and he screams and shouts and wonders why that happened to him. It's that tantrum he throws because he couldn't challenge Smith back then. So he is kind of stuck there because little Larry wasn't supposed to be rude to priests, and he had to take whatever it was he took and he wasn't allowed to react.

I was talking to him one morning recently and I said, "You know, one of the things they teach you in rape prevention classes is to fight back. If your reaction is to throw up on the attacker or pee on him, you do it. You do whatever you have to do."

He had been a policeman for three years and he said that he had never heard that, and then he said, "Oh my God, I should have done that. I might have stopped it."

But he couldn't have stopped it because of his upbringing. He was taught that priests couldn't and wouldn't do anything wrong. But Smith did do something wrong, and he told Larry he couldn't tell anyone about it.

Smith effectively severed those ties of trust that little Larry had in his parents to protect him. It didn't matter whether they knew or not. They could not have known, but that's not the point. The child in Larry knew that his parents were there to protect him, and they didn't. They couldn't. That happened at such a crucial stage of his development. Adolescence is so wonky anyway under normal circumstances. I can't even begin to imagine what has gone on in his mind.

Up until eight years ago Larry was still going to church. Things started getting worse in 2002 when the abuse stories started breaking in Boston. It was when the U.S. Conference of Catholic Bishops met that year that the torment accelerated. By 2006, things had gotten out of hand.

In September of that year Larry started having more rage. It was a newspaper article that he had read, and his rage started spiraling. It was on September 15, 2006, that things really fell apart.

I had read an article or something that said the archdiocese was helping sexual abuse victims with money, therapy and medication. I called the archdiocese and they put me through to Wayne Pribble, their victim's assistance coordinator. He said he was going to need to interview Larry. He asked me to have Larry call him, which Larry did. Larry called and Pribble said he was going to have to come into the archdiocese's office and tell his story. He told Larry that that was the only way they could help him. Larry told him that he needed help and that he wasn't part of the original lawsuits, and he said, "You know this man did it. He's already been sued and you settled."

But Pribble said they needed documentation and that they needed to talk. By that time I was on the phone again with Pribble, and Larry was in the study, and the next thing I knew, Larry had a phone book in his hand and was ripping it to pieces. Then he picked up a blue chair and slammed it onto the coffee table. He went upstairs and I found him banging his head into the wall outside on our balcony.

I called Sergeant Pat and told him that Larry was one of those who had been abused by priests and that he was trying to get help from the Church. I told him that Larry was throwing furniture and hurting himself. By the time Pat got to the house, Larry was out of it. Pat said, "Come on buddy, we need to get you checked out."

Larry wouldn't get into the ambulance that came over, and so Pat let him ride in the front seat of the squad car and took him to Kaseman Hospital. Pat called me about three-thirty in the morning and said he had gotten Larry checked in.

I called Larry later that morning at the hospital and said I was coming to pick him up. He said not to bother. I drove the seven miles to the hospital and asked for Larry. Someone there said that he had already left. I drove around and around and found Larry walking down the street and tried to get him into the car. I kept pulling into parking lots and saying, "Please get into the car. You're hurting yourself."

Larry had had a compound fracture of his ankle in 2004 and it didn't heal properly, and for a year he had bone showing where there should have been skin.

At one point I told Larry, "Your leg isn't healed all the way, get in the car." He refused and I gave up. Larry eventually got home. He didn't talk to me for three days after that.

We all knew that Larry needed help, and at that point his family wrote a letter to Sheehan asking him to please do something. They thought it would work because Larry's father was close to the Church and to the archbishop. Sheehan smoked cigars and came into the shop regularly. The family said that Larry wasn't part of the original lawsuits that had been filed in the early 1990s, and they pleaded for help. It was a really good letter.

That led to October 13, 2006, when Larry was in the shop and got that phone call from Sheehan. That's when we found him in the alley burning himself and banging his head into the metal door.

We got Larry to Kaseman again and he was diagnosed with PTSD. He stayed there five days. That's when we sent him to The Meadows for thirty days.

Larry went into Kaseman that Friday. I had to take one of our sons to his soccer game on Saturday and I was barely functioning. I called a friend and said, "I just have to talk." I told her about everything. She said she would make some phone calls to people she knew who knew about priest sex abuse and PTSD. She called me back fifteen minutes later and gave me an 800 number for The Meadows. I called and talked to someone and explained the situation and they said they could handle it.

I asked them, "How fast can we get him there?"

The guy on the phone said the intake people would be there on Monday, but he took all the information over the phone. I called them back on Monday morning. Larry came home from Kaseman on Tuesday night, and on Wednesday morning he and his brother Dan were flying to Arizona for Larry's thirty-day stay.

I don't think The Meadows was much fun for Larry, what with having to relive all that horror and terror. It was hard on us at home. Larry was gone and I had to run the shop, get the kids to school and soccer practice and games and run the household and wonder if Larry was getting better, or if he ever would. I thought of our kids. We have five, and they've always known that there was something wrong with their dad. What do you tell them when their dad is gone for a month? What do you tell them? How do you tell them that their father was raped by a Catholic priest when he was fifteen?

It's not much fun knowing that your husband is undergoing thirty days of intensive, inpatient treatment at a place five hundred miles away. All you do is wonder, hope, pray and worry about him. Will he ever get better? Will he heal, at least a little? What's going to happen to the shop, to me, to Larry and to the family?

I think it was the day we got Larry to The Meadows that Larry's father, Larry Sr., wrote Archbishop Sheehan a letter asking for help for his son.

Sheehan responded on October 23, 2006, with a letter that said:

"I am deeply saddened for Larry and keep him and the family in prayer.

"I said on the phone the other day that I want to help in the counseling expenses that you mentioned. As I agreed in our phone conversation, I am enclosing a check for $15,000 to assist.

"I am one with you in the hope that we can resolve an amicable solution to this tragedy.

"Sincerely yours in the Risen Lord."

That's all the Church ever seems to want to do in these cases, settle them in an amicable matter.

If they want to be "amicable," why are they still harboring rapists and not turning them over to authorities? Why don't they apologize to all these victims and ask for their forgiveness? Why don't they do that?

Larry seemed to do well at The Meadows, but the people there said he needed more intensive treatment, like three months worth. They said if he didn't get it he wouldn't recover fully and would eventually have another breakdown. We found a place in Florida and made arrangements for Larry to go, and he was going to go, but then we got word that his father's cancer had returned and that it was terminal.

We decided that we had to tell Larry, and he made the decision to cancel that treatment and care for his dad. His father died on July 16, 2007.

Larry didn't go to Florida. It might have helped him. Instead, he began to decline again. Every time he heard or read about how the Church wasn't fully addressing this issue he got angry.

He came back from a fishing trip not too long ago. It was a Thursday, and he turned on the TV or read the newspaper or something and it was just too much. It was overload.

He looked down at the paper in disgust and said, "I can't do this anymore. The kids are set up, the shop is doing well. I'm leaving."

"Where are you going?" I asked.

"I don't know," he replied. Then he took out his credit card and his gas card and his driver's license and took off. That was about five in the afternoon.

I called Sergeant Pat and asked if he was on duty and told him that Larry had left. He asked if Larry had taken his motorcycle or car. I said, "No, he's walking."

Pat said, "He'll be back. It's supposed to get down to thirty degrees tonight. He'll be back."

I had visions of Larry walking to Annunciation and knocking out the church's windows or something. I knew it was going to be a long night.

Larry called about ten-thirty and said he was at a Wal-Mart and asked me to come and pick him up. I did. I didn't know where he had been, but I doubt he was in Wal-Mart for five hours. When I picked him up he said, "Sometimes I just need to do that."

It was rough while Larry was at The Meadows. I had to keep things going. I was running around like a maniac worrying about Larry, worrying about the kids and the shop and just worrying about everything.

One day I was up in our bedroom and I took a step forward and looked down and there was no floor in front of me, just a deep black hole. I froze. I was terrified. If I took another step I would have fallen into the abyss. I was going crazy.

Somehow I got control, leaned back against the bedroom wall, closed my eyes, and took some deep breaths and prayed like I hadn't prayed in a while. Instead of trying to get through Larry's situation on my own strength, I was reminded that God's strength was all I ever need. At that moment, I, spiritually and emotionally, climbed into God's lap and stayed there until I saw Larry walking towards me at the Albuquerque airport when he returned from Arizona. The black hole disappeared and I walked out and got on with things.

Larry has had trouble concentrating and staying with things. In the past six years he's had six cars and four motorcycles. He hates staying in hotels. He won't take his socks off when he's in one. He remembers the sickening, dirty, shag carpets and the sticky bathroom floors. He gets sick if he drives by Annunciation or to Clovis. He won't go to Carlsbad.

One year our daughter wanted to go to Carlsbad Caverns. I thought it would be a good idea. We've got an RV, so Larry would not have had to stay in a hotel. Then I remembered that Smith took him there. I mentioned the idea of the trip to Larry and he just said, "I don't really want to go to Carlsbad right now. The caverns are beautiful, and I would like for the kids to see them, but not right now."

"Sexual abuse doesn't just blow up the person who was abused; it blows up everyone around them. And so long as that person doesn't get help, it keeps blowing up and blowing up and blowing up and hurting every one you deal with."—Larry Monte Jr.

Eight

Institutionalized

This chapter should really be called "In the Nuthouse," because that's where I landed on October 13, 2006, after I had burned my hands and arms with a cigar and slammed and slammed and slammed my head into that metal door down the alley from the cigar shop.

It's an interesting experience to bang your head into a metal door. The metal usually gives, that is, if it isn't too thick and if it's a hollow door, which most of them are, and you can put a dent in it. It feels good to be able to dent something, even if it's just with your skull. If that door had been pure and solid steel, hell, even solid wood, my skull would have cracked and my brain would have oozed out in a sloppy mess onto the ground, and the flies and bugs and ants would have devoured it and I would have been gone.

That is what I wanted. The door didn't cooperate. It was one of those hollow things, tin-plated if you ask me, and I was reduced to putting dents in it instead of it cracking open my head and letting my brain slide out onto the asphalt-paved alley and letting the bugs eat my shame and guilt and worth-lessness away.

That's what I wanted. I wanted to be rid of this brain and these memories. I wanted an army of ants to swarm over my slimy, bloody, filthy mess of a brain and eat it. I wanted cock-roaches to crawl all over that brain with their thin, black and brown legs and despicable mouths and eat it. I wanted centi-pedes, and god knows what other tiny creatures there are, to eat it and shit it out.

That's not too healthy a thought pattern and so I wound up in Kaseman Hospital's psych ward where I was laced into a straitjacket and pumped full of sedatives. No matter how many drugs they put into me they didn't have much of an effect. I wanted out of the place. I didn't think I belonged there. I didn't think I was crazy. I didn't think I belonged in a straitjacket.

You know what it's like being in a straitjacket? Your arms are tied. You can't move them. If someone tries punching you in the face or stomach you can't get your arms free to block the blows, let alone swing back. If someone goes to kick you in the balls you can't move and cross your arms to protect yourself. You're totally defenseless and at the mercy of everyone! That's a total lack of control over yourself. That's vulnerability. That's how I felt with Smith, and there in Kaseman, in that straitjacket, that's how I felt again. I was helpless, and I was hopeless. I was full of drugs and in a psych ward. I was going crazy. No, I had already gone crazy.

Here's the insane thing about it. I had just pounded my head into a metal door and burned my hands and arms with a cigar and I didn't think I was crazy or needed help. That's denial.

It was the closest thing to being in prison that I know of and it was the lowest point in my life. I was humiliated.

They took my belt, the drawstrings on my sweats and eve-rything else I could use to hang myself. I couldn't have a razor. We had plastic spoons and forks to eat with. My room had a window with bars on it that looked out to a fenced courtyard lined with barbed wire. There was no what I call real food, just finger food and sandwiches. I had to get permission to get a razor and shave, and when I did shave, they had someone with me to watch. They let us into the courtyard, but only without our shoes so we wouldn't run away. We had to line up in the mornings at a window to get our medications. About the only freedom we had was to choose what to eat at meal times. That was simple. I think I ate fourteen hamburgers in my five days there. We had to see a shrink every day. That first night I was tied with restraints by my wrists and ankles to the rails of my bed. I was lying there on my back looking up at the ceiling and thinking, "What the fuck have I done? What have I become?"

We were pretty much escorted everywhere we went. We got to roam the halls during the day and talk with other inmates, but I didn't talk to anyone. I didn't think I was crazy like they were.

Here's the most humiliating thing about it. They didn't give us anything to do or to play with or to keep us occupied except crayons and coloring books. I felt like an idiot.

It was at Kaseman Hospital that I was diagnosed with Posttraumatic Stress Disorder. As I now know, that was the proper diagnosis.

As horrible and as humiliating as that stay was, it was good for me. It was there that I knew I had to get help and get myself well. Jean visited me twice a day. My dad called and urged me to get help and said he would do anything to get me that help.

At one point I realized that I had turned into my greatest fear. I had broken down and gone crazy. That's when I thought to myself, "Is this going to be my legacy? Being in a nuthouse? Is this the memory of myself I'm going to leave my wife and my kids? A guy who bangs his head into doors, burns himself, tries hanging himself, flies into rages, throws furniture, smashes dishes, sulks, broods, disappears on long walks, shouts, screams and walks around every day in a self-pitying funk?"

Up to then everything was maddening. Absolutely maddening. Me and people like me get trapped in our own heads. No one understands what you're going through. No one understands the pain, the shame the sense of worthlessness and the torment. You're alone with all that pain in a tiny space in your head and it's torture. You hear the voices that say you're a piece of shit and worthless, and you feel the pain inside your head. You try to explain it to people, and when you look at them it's like looking at tree full of owls. You just get blank stares and slow blinks because they don't understand. How can they?

Then you retreat more and more into yourself and it becomes even more maddening and painful, and you just want to scream and scream and scream some more and bust open your head to relieve the pain and scrub your brain clean. You just want to scrub the filth and the pain off. You think that if you could just wash it with soap and water the pain and the torment will vanish.

It won't, though. It won't.

I was also one of those tough guys who thought that psychological help was for losers and wusses. Real men don't go to shrinks. We just suck up the pain and the torment and move on. I thought I had moved on, but being locked up in a psych ward in a room with crayons and coloring books knocked that dumb thought out of me fast.

My failure to get help and deal with this before then was selfish. I lied to my family. I lied to my friends. I lied to my colleagues. I lied to myself. You lie because that's the only thing you think you've got. That's how hopeless and bleak and dark and painful the situation is. You lie, you know you're lying, you don't want to lie, but you can't stop yourself from lying and hurting yourself and others. It's an unending circle of unbearable pain, torment and destruction. Mutilating yourself, you know, pounding your head into a door or wall or burning yourself, distracts you from the pain in your head. I burned myself because it made me forget, at least for a little while, about the pain in my head.

It is selfish and it is destructive to everyone around you. That's what I want to make clear about being raped by a priest. The physical acts and the torment haven't just affected me. It has hurt everyone around me and with whom I deal. It's like a bomb exploding. A bomb hits its target, but the explosion blows out windows in other buildings, spews shrapnel that hits and injures people, starts fires that rage out of control, and severs sewer, gas and water lines, which start more fires and hurt more people.

Sexual abuse doesn't just blow up the person who was abused; it blows up everyone around them. And so long as that person doesn't get help, it keeps blowing up and blowing up and blowing up and hurting every one you deal with.

That's why I so hate your organization. You don't understand that, you don't recognize and admit it, and you don't want to. Your raping men of God have destroyed the lives of tens of thousands, probably hundreds of thousands, of kids in this country, as well as the lives of the hundreds and hundreds of thousands of people they deal with. The path of destruction is so wide and so great, but you reduce it to statistics. You care only about your organization, image, rules, privilege and control. You don't care about the millions of lives you've destroyed.

If you did care you would turn the rapists over to the law to make sure they're prosecuted and that they rot in prison. If you cared you would burn your Canon Law, end your secrecy, admit your crimes and sins and hold yourselves to the same standards that you demand of your sheep. If you cared you would seek justice and show kindness, love and compassion to us, not just to members of your club. If you cared, you would behave in a Christlike way, rage at the child rapists and cleanse your temples and gilded palaces of the vipers, snakes and devils.

You don't because you don't care about God's precious children and their trusting souls. You don't because you're the farthest thing from Christ than anyone can imagine. You're the opposite of Christ. You know what that makes you, don't you?

Up until that second stay at Kaseman I was still blaming myself for all of this. I blamed myself for having led a man of God to sin. I was in a state of self-pity where everything was my fault, and nothing was going to convince me otherwise. I thought that everything that happened to me was something that I deserved because of my failures. I deserved what I was getting and what I had gotten for having partaken in that filth in those motel rooms.

Think of the lunacy of it. My fault? I was fifteen when it began. Smith was in his forties. I, a fifteen-year-old boy, seduced a man in his forties? That's how sick and twisted this stuff becomes and that's how vile it is. That's how your organization made and makes us feel.

Something clicked in those four or five days, and I realized that I had to get over my own selfishness. I had to stop hurting myself and all of those around me.

I'm proud that I was able to finally see that. What I'm most proud of my second visit to Kaseman, though, is this:

I refused to play with the crayons.

****

Immediately after I got out of Kaseman I flew to Wickenburg, Arizona, and The Meadows treatment center for a thirty-day stay. It was better than Kaseman. It was dormitory-style facility with spacious grounds. I had two roommates, and we had our own bathroom in the room. That was a luxury.

The humiliating thing about being in the loony bin is what they take from you and how you lose your freedom. After checking in I got my bags back. Gone were my razors, my medications and even a pack of chewing gum. The everyday freedoms you take for granted are taken from you. If I wanted to shave I had to get permission from my shrink and check out a razor. For the first four or five days I wasn't allowed to shave. Maybe they were afraid I'd nick myself.

We were free to roam the grounds, but I had to sign an agreement that said that if I wandered off those grounds I'd be kicked out of the program and sent home. From the standpoint of physical comfort it was great. We were allowed in the swimming pool for an hour every day. Men and women were not allowed to mingle. It was a highly controlled and tightly monitored place.

I was assigned a shrink and had to go to group counseling every day. You went to meetings twice a day and then you had a number of lectures to attend and various assignments you had to produce throughout the course of the day. They wanted us to get in touch with our higher power. That was strange to me because I always thought the higher power was God.

I was assigned another counselor for my spiritual healing. He was a portly and elderly guy. Can't remember his name, but I was enjoying talking with him. I told him that I was there because I had been raped by a priest. He was very empathetic and said how it was an evil thing and how the Catholic Church was an evil institution. I was getting to like him because he seemed to really get what rape-by-priest was about. He was telling me what I wanted to hear.

It was my fourth or fifth day there and toward the end of one of our sessions when he said there was one thing he needed to tell me. He had just finished blasting the Catholic Church when he said, "I'm a Catholic priest."

"Holy crap," I thought to myself, "here I am again, in the presence of another fat priest. What the hell is this guy going to try?"

Then he said that I needed to keep it a secret and not tell anyone because none of the other patients were supposed to know that he was a priest. If they did, they might not feel comfortable going to him for spiritual help and guidance.

"Here we go again," I thought. "This guy's ashamed of what he is and what he belongs to, and now he's asking me to keep his dirty secret."

It was Smith all over again in a way. I had another SOB, another Catholic priest, wanting me to keep a secret.

From that point on my healing didn't progress very well. I told management what the guy had told me, and they said they were outraged. They said they were going to talk to and reprimand him, and maybe they did, but I always saw him walking around the place. I didn't go to him after that.

My spiritual healing was supposed to be a large part of the overall healing, and that had just vanished for me.

Most of the patients that I talked with were there for alcohol and drug addictions. There was one other guy who had been raped by a priest, and we became friends and leaned on each other. He was married, had a seven-year-old daughter and was an accomplished attorney. He had argued before the U.S. Supreme Court and was just an accomplished guy. As did I, he had a constant mental battle going on in his head, and we understood each other.

After we left The Meadows, a few of us kept in touch, and about a year later I got an email saying that the attorney had hanged himself by throwing himself off a bridge. I went crazy again. All I could think about was the destruction this stuff has caused. Imagine his wife and how destroyed she must have felt. Imagine his daughter and how she must have felt when told that her father had hanged himself. They will never heal from that. Never.

How about all the deaths from alcohol and drug overdoses these child-raping priests have caused? How about the divorces, the people in prison, the lost homes and the lost lives because of this sickening mess?

A man put a rope around his neck and jumped off a bridge because of being raped by a Catholic priest. And all you vile people can say is that you've addressed the problem and that you won't turn the child rapists over to the law?

All you can do is give cavalier lip service to the fact that a man put a rope around his neck and jumped of a bridge and left his wife and young daughter husbandless and fatherless? You pigs!

I don't want another child ever hurt like this again. That's why I'm writing this. I hope that this anguish and this horror and this torment and this pain might cause someone, somewhere in you sick, twisted organization to somehow grow a brain, a heart and a soul and say that this has to be stopped once and for all and forever and all time.

Is there one of you who can do that? Just one?

I can only imagine how things would be if people the world over and in your club had spoken out ferociously and unrelentingly a hundred years ago and stopped the child-raping priests. I would not have been raped. My lawyer friend would still be alive. His wife would still have a husband, and his daughter a loving father. But no! No! You protected the rapists and your organization and continued to let the criminals take children and rape and rape and rape them some more.

Can you even figure out a little why so many people think your club should be destroyed and banished from the earth forever? Do you at all get that?

I'm not so naïve as to think that one man screaming in unrelenting, pain, anger and torment for a couple hundred pages in a book will change anything, let alone the world, but I am hopeful, otherwise there would be no use in living.

This has to end and it has to end now, this moment.

I never want another child to be hurt like this again, and I vow to do all I can and never stop until that's a reality.

Hey princes of the Church, how about you?

"The bishop said he was surprised by my statement, as he said he thought that Larry had gotten over it and there was no longer a problem."—Anthony Contri

Nine

Invaded

Here's Jean again to tell you about another sickening event in this sordid tale:

It was in April of this year (2010), the week that Larry started on this book, that the most amazing and awful thing happened. It was right around tax day, and we were in the shop and the cigar club. Larry was coming up the stairs from the club's lower level and two older guys were going down the stairs. It's a three-foot-wide stairway with six stairs, and Larry was just starting up when they passed each other. One of the guys—he was in a sports shirt and slacks—extended his hand out to Larry and said, "Hey, how are you?" Larry, out of instinct, shook it.

When Larry got to the top of the stairs and walked into the retail shop his face was white. All the blood had drained out of it. He was in shock.

I knew that something was wrong and I wondered what could have happened between the six stairs and the main floor.

Larry walked straight out of the shop and out to the parking lot. I followed him and he said, "Do you know who that was?" I said I didn't.

"That was the archbishop. That was Sheehan. I feel like I need to go throw up." he said. Then he got into his car and drove away. I thought he was going to run the car into a wall and kill himself or something. He was in such shock.

I left to go make a bank deposit and I started driving down San Mateo Boulevard. I drove for a few minutes and then, being outraged myself, I turned around and went back to the shop because I was going to throw the archbishop out. What was he doing in our shop? And what was he doing there the week that Larry started on the book?

I was furious. I got back to the store and our son Matt was there. He helps run the place. Matt said that the archbishop and the priest with him were downstairs in a smoking room. I walked down the stairs to the smoking rooms and I was trembling with rage. I was going to throw that creep out. He had just hurt my husband—again!

When I got downstairs I saw that a lawyer friend ours, Anthony Contri, was talking to Sheehan and the other guy. Anthony was there because he was supposed to meet Larry so they could moan and groan over tax day with cigars. I walked over to Anthony and said, "Anthony, do you need some help?"

He said, "Jean, I've got this under control."

Here's Anthony's version of what happened:

> On a Friday afternoon in early 2010, I had arranged with Larry to meet him at his cigar shop at four in the afternoon to discuss the upcoming governor's race.
>
> As I arrived at his store, I saw his son Matt behind the counter and asked where his dad was hiding out. It was immediately obvious from the look on Matt's

face that something was wrong. He said, "He's not here. He just left."

I responded by asking what was wrong, and he looked at me in a panic and said, "The bishop is here with another priest." He informed me that his dad had to leave because he was so upset that the bishop and the priest had just waltzed in and acted as though nothing had ever happened.

I knew immediately why Larry had left. From past conversations with Larry, I knew he had significant disdain for the bishop. The bishop had told Larry in their last meeting that he "just needed to get over it," as it happened a long time ago and that he had had nothing to do with it. Aside from the obvious callousness of the comment, Larry felt the bishop had significantly misstated the truth, as the bishop had been called upon to clean up the mess, and in doing so had been complicit in sequestering some of the priests involved in order to protect them from prosecution, and his motives were to protect the Church, not to help in the healing of the victims. The hypocrisy of this unnerved Larry and he had told me that if he ever saw him again he was afraid that he would just physically smash him, as he represented all the evil of the past. Luckily for the bishop, Larry had the good judgment to leave.

Matt told me that he was waiting for his mother to return to operate the register so he could go down to the smoking room and ask the bishop to leave before his father returned. I asked Matt which room the bishop and the priest were in, as I wanted to go see for myself what was really going on. I walked to the room Matt had indicated, looked inside and saw the bishop with another priest sitting and smoking cigars. I returned back upstairs and suggested to Matt that he should let me handle the matter. He seemed relieved and asked if he could watch. I suggested that it would be better that he stay and watch the register until his mother returned.

I asked Matt how they had managed to get downstairs. He told me he had rushed them down to the room as soon as he saw his father's reaction to them entering the shop; as he was afraid of what was going to happen. I thought to myself how lucky for the bishop that Matt had acted so swiftly. I also thought, "What have I just volunteered to do?" Having attended Catholic schools all my pre-college years, I had a lot of thoughts rushing through my head as I walked downstairs to the smoking room.

I walked into the room with the two men and sat down on a sofa directly across from them and waited for a break in their discussion. I guess the look on my face transmitted to them that I had entered the room for a reason, as they stopped talking almost immediately. I looked at the bishop, and then the priest sitting to his right and introduced myself. They then introduced themselves, at which point I learned that the priest sitting with the bishop was a monsignor of the church. At this point, for some reason, it ran through my head that I was now playing a live game of chess with both a knight and a bishop rather than a pawn and a bishop, in this little discussion that was about to take place, and it seemed to raise the bar. I had no idea what piece I was or what position I held on the board. The thought quickly left me and I just opened my mouth and asked the bishop if he really thought it was a good idea that he was here, considering all that had occurred in Larry's life.

The monsignor at this point gave me a kind of death stare, which for some spiritual reason, caused a rush of conviction as to why I was there at that moment. It was profoundly empowering. I looked back at him and asked, as though he had just stepped into a pile of muck, if he had any confusion about what I was referring to, as I was quite certain that the bishop was aware of what I meant, and that I would be glad to explain it in detail if he needed me to. He turned meek and said he had some idea about what I was referring to, though he did not know all of the details. I offered again to explain, at which point he stated that it was not necessary. The bishop concurred.

The bishop said he was surprised by my statement, as he said he thought that Larry had gotten over it and there was no longer a problem. I told him that I was surprised that he could have that impression, as I was certain that the one person who could have told him that, never has. I continued that I wondered how he thought Larry could have gotten over it. He responded, defending the fact that they were in the smoking room as he and the monsignor had been invited to come down to the smoking room as soon as they had arrived and that I was wrong in my assertion.

I told him that I thought that he completely misunderstood what had actually had gone on upon his arrival. I pointed out the obvious, that it was not Larry who had ushered him downstairs, but his son, Matt, who had felt he had to take that action to avert an otherwise potentially explosive situation. I asked him to acknowledge that my statement of how the events had just unfolded was correct, and that perhaps he was in error in his interpretation of the events. He asked if I thought he had done this intentionally to anger Larry. I told him I was not asserting that, though I wondered if it was not done without considering how it might affect Larry, given what had happened to him. I also told the bishop that if I thought he had done it deliberately to provoke Larry, I would be having a very different conversation with him. He got my point.

The bishop then asked me how he was supposed to know that Larry was still upset. I told him that to categorize it as "upset" seemed as though he did not fully grasp the situation and that there are some things that happen in life that people just don't ever "get over."

At this point the monsignor stated he understood the situation and that he was sorry they had come, but then again, asked if I thought they had done it deliberately. I again stated that was not my assertion and that if it was, we would not be having such a "civil" conversation. He looked at me like the kid in class who just asked the teacher a question that had just been answered when he wasn't paying attention. I was a little annoyed at this point and could not help myself. I asked him again if he needed me to cover the details of Larry's past. I then stated that their visit seemed not to require prior knowledge on their part, that it might not be a good idea, as they had the facts to deduce that themselves.

The bishop interrupted and said he had done nothing to Larry and did not even know Larry when it happened to him. I was taken a little back by this comment, and, looking at the bishop, I took some time to explain how he was directly involved when he was given the job of clean-up and (calling upon my earlier education) asked if he did not recognize that in his position, he was, in fact, the walking symbol of the

Catholic Church in New Mexico as the bishop of the archdiocese?

I tried to explain to him that he should understand the visceral reaction that Larry had to seeing him, as, to Larry, he was a walking representation of the evil that had invaded his young life. He asked what I was asking of him, to which I said that I thought it best that he leave and not ever again return to the shop. He then asked if I was saying that no one associated with the Church was welcome there. I told him that was not what I was saying, but that specifically, he should not return, and again asked if he could not understand that, with the position he holds in the Church, his very presence causes a very real, visceral pain in Larry, and potentially other victims. He indicated he was not sure why I would say that, and that he did not see how he was guilty of anything that happened to Larry. I realized that repeating myself on this point was, in fact, pointless.

He asked if he needed to leave immediately. I told him to feel free to finish his cigar and then it would be best if he left. As I stood up to leave, he asked me if I needed anything else. I stopped, sat down, looked at him and said, "Yes." He asked, "What?" and I told him that I, like many others who had been raised Catholic, would like to know how the Church could have repeatedly responded so poorly to what happened on so many occasions to so many children. I told him how I could understand how it could have happened that an individual priest could have acted so badly, but how did the Church decide to make the same mistake over and over again? He said, "Do we really need to get into this?" I responded, "No. No we don't. I can just leave and continue to wonder, like so many others just like me, how this could happen and how, just like right now, the Church could repeatedly respond so poorly."

I got up and left the room.

I went upstairs to explain what had taken place to Matt. His first question to me was, "Are they leaving?" I told him they were and that I did not think they would return. He thanked me and I asked him where I could find his father. I then left to go find my friend, his father. As I drove away, I was struck at how significantly grateful I felt, that I had the chance to help in such a small way, and that I now had a better understanding of what Larry had been dealing with all these years.

Jean continues:

After talking with Anthony I phoned home to see if Larry was there. Our son Patrick said he wasn't and he asked what was wrong. I told him that the archbishop had come into the shop and that Larry had seen him and that he had gotten upset.

I hated to tell Patrick that because I know how his stomach gets upset when he knows that Larry is angry. I called Larry on his cell phone. He was in a bar with a couple of guys from the store and he was okay. It was a hell of a day.

The good thing about that day is that Larry removed himself from the situation and that he didn't hurt himself like he had done in the past. I'm sure he wanted to kill Sheehan.

I got home and Larry was there. We had—and I say we used to have—a three-foot-tall, stone statue of St. Francis on the side of the house next to the driveway. Larry went out to the driveway, picked up the statue, raised it over his head and smashed it onto the concrete. St. Francis wound up in hundreds of pieces.

I don't think that Church officials, Sheehan included, know what happens in the homes of the people their priests have raped. They don't know what happens to the families and the marriages. They just say, "Here's a check and it's over. We'll pray for you, and by the way, you have to return to the sacraments."

What is wrong with them?

I love Larry. I made a promise to God and to him that I will always be with him, and I will. I can't imagine life without him and I don't want to imagine life without him. Every time things get bad, I know that "this too will pass."

The thing that gets me about all these cases, past and present, is why did those bishops never call the police? Why can't they just pick up the phone and say, "We have parents here who say that their child has been hurt by this priest. Can you come and pick him up?"

Why, why did they not pick up the phone and say that a child had been hurt in their parish? Child rape is a crime.

Why, why, why did they never call the police on those monsters?

Here's Larry again:

"Even though the abusive relationship is terribly damaging to the victim, he finds it difficult to remove himself from it because of the priest's power over him and the psychological and emotional bond that has resulted."—Philadelphia Grand Jury Report, September, 2005.

Ten

Twisted

Dear Slobs:

Being raped by a priest at a young age—we know that our brains aren't fully developed until age twenty-five—really screws you up. I've told you about the shame and the guilt and the agony and the misery and the grief and the feeling that I'm a worthless piece of garbage who's not fit for life. Well, listen to this: I was so screwed up, so never wanting this to come out, so wanting to take this evil secret to my grave, so afraid and so terrified of anyone knowing this that I let the perverted, fat, smelly, diabetic, child-raping Smith marry Jean and me.

That's right, I let that pig marry us.

We were both twenty-two. We had met at the University of New Mexico. I had started there in 1976. We were friends at first. Jean was dating one of my frat brothers and was living in the sorority house where I worked as a waiter and cleaner. The job earned me meals. One of the women there had a crush on me, I guess, and Jean set me up with her. That didn't work out.

Jean and I actually started dating in March or April of 1979. She was from Beaumont, Texas, and I did like her accent, among other things.

Smith was still bugging me—calling to complain about his advancing diabetes, going on and on about the joys of masturbation and wanting to meet and drink beer. All I wanted was to get out of Albuquerque and away from him.

By that time I was getting a drafting certificate from what is now Central New Mexico Community College. It was called Albuquerque Technical Vocational Institute back then, and Jean and I had gotten engaged and had set the wedding for June of 1980.

In the summer of 1979, Jean moved to Austin to help care for her sister, who had breast cancer. She returned to UNM in August, and at the end of October, I was offered a job as a draftsman by the Huber Corporation in Borger, Texas, a small, truly depressing town a little north of Amarillo.

I took the job and took off for the great metropolis of Borger.

Borger was famous, if you can call it that, for the manufacture of t-butyl mercaptan, the chemical that's put into natural gas to give it its smell. T-butyl, as we called it, smells a lot like rotten cabbage, and I had the brains to take a crummy, one-bedroom apartment across the street from the t-butyl plant.

They injected the t-butyl into the gas pipelines that ran through Borger. The town had about 10,000 people. It was basically a giant chemical plant and was dirty, dry, hot, and had hardly any trees. If you go on its website today you'll find that it has exactly three things for tourists to do. I guess that's better than none. Its cop car, or at least one of them, was an old Gremlin.

They also made Carbon Black in Borger. That's a fine, fine powder that's used in tires and other things. There was no way back then, and I'm sure even today, to keep the stuff from getting all over town. Everything about Borger had a thin, black film to it. It got on your skin, through the window sills, where it would pile up in little ridges, and on your clothes.

That's where I brought Jean. My god, I owe that woman. She deserves a special crown on her head.

I used to go into the t-butyl plant once a week to look at equipment. Then I'd go back later to Huber and draw the stuff. The stench of that place was so intense that every time I walked out of my tiny apartment I felt like throwing up.

There wasn't anything to do in Borger but drink. An older guy I worked with felt sorry for me, I guess, and would often take me to Red's tavern where we would drink beer and eat calf fries—which are nothing but deep-fried steer balls. I didn't have much money, and my friend usually paid. That was kind of him.

One day the t-butyl plant exploded. It blew out the windows of my apartment.

I worked nights and weekends at the town's gravel pit—drove a bulldozer. That paid more than the draftsman's work. But it was somewhat unpleasant as it seemed that I had to stop every three or four minutes to empty my shoes of stones. I went to the Catholic Church there, as I was still hooked into the organization. It wasn't much fun. The priest had a speech impediment, and I could never understand him. His sermons were unintelligible. He said mass in about fifteen minutes. On Sundays he took his time and got through mass in twenty minutes.

I felt sorry for the guy and always wondered what he had done wrong to get assigned to Borger, Texas, the t-butyl mercaptan capital of the U.S.

I came home at Thanksgiving and told Jean that I couldn't take living in Borger by myself—no one could—and we moved the wedding date to January 11, 1980.

Ma and Dad were happy, and one of the first things out of Ma's mouth was that Smith—good old raping Fr. Robert John Smith—had to marry us. After all he was a family friend and the "mentor" who had groomed me for the priesthood, among other things.

Smith probably expected to be asked to do the wedding. Although I was horrified and disgusted by the idea, I went along with it because I was terrified of my past and of him. I was scared to death of letting anyone else in the Catholic Church do it.

Why?

Because I was afraid that he was going to go public with this. He used to use it against me all the time. I didn't want anybody to know. He was a man of God, which I ridiculously still believed. All I ever heard over and over again was how he was a man of God. I thought that if I didn't let him do the marriage, he would tell my parents everything. And knowing that pig, I figured he'd say it was all my fault, that I seduced him and caused a man of God to sin and that I enjoyed every minute of that filth with him in those cheesy motel rooms. I didn't, of course. I hated it all, each and every sickening moment of it. That's how twisted my mind was. I thought that Smith would say that I grabbed his hand during those "wonderful" moments in the church sacristy before going out to serve mass and stuck it on my balls.

Yeah, that's what I thought he would say, that it was all my fault.

Can you imagine what would have happened had I gotten a different priest for the wedding? Everyone in the family would have asked all sorts of questions, things like, "Why won't you let him marry you?" and on and on. I didn't want to go there, and so it was just easier to let him marry us.

Of course, I introduced Jean to him. I'll stop here and let Jean give you her impressions of your man of God.

Here's Jean again:

Smith was a pig, I mean, he was pig-like. He was very porcine with a bald head, fat face, squinty eyes, and he smelled like beer every time I was around him. It was gross. He cussed a lot. I didn't understand Larry's family letting him into their home and letting him be around their children.

They're such a gracious and well-mannered family, so why Smith? In hindsight, now, I think that's exactly how Smith weaseled his way into their family. He played on their graciousness, respect for clergy, and, I believe, their sympathy for him as a "poor servant of the Church, living alone, with no family." It was an Oscar-worthy performance, and Larry was his prize.

There have been several instances since his parents learned the truth that Larry's mom has berated herself and asked me, "How did I not know? Why didn't I see what was going on?"

The only response I could think of was, "That's how good Smith was at his 'job' of manipulation and deceit." That was his life's purpose, to lie his way into victims' homes and families as the New Mexico Catholic Church cleared a path for him. Smith knew exactly what he was doing, and, sadly, so did the Catholic Church.

Smith would go over to their house and tell off-color jokes and use foul language, and Larry's parents would laugh. It was like, "Wink, wink. Isn't that Father Smith something?" And they'd nudge each other and look the other way.

I wasn't raised Catholic, and I had a "discussion" with Smith about the contradictions of his religion and its teachings and beliefs, especially about the Virgin Mary.

I had arguments—make that discussions—with Larry about it too. Once we talked about Mary and I said that she had had other kids and that I didn't buy the perpetual virgin teaching. I said, "She married Joseph and they had other kids, it's in scripture. What's this perpetual virgin thing?"

"Oh, no," Larry said. "You need to talk to Smith."

So I made an appointment to meet Smith—in a pizza joint/bar. He drank his beer that day.

I said something like, "Mary had other kids."

"No she didn't," he replied. "It's in the Bible."

I told him he was wrong and asked him, "What is it about brothers and sisters that you don't understand?" This was his brilliant response:

"Oh, they're talking about brothers and sisters in Christ."

The discussion with Smith didn't go well. Afterwards, he told Larry that he shouldn't marry me, and that if he did, the marriage wouldn't last more than two years.

I didn't want Smith to marry us, but he was the family priest, and so I figured that I'd go along with it and not make any waves. I have no idea where our wedding album is. Smith's picture was in it, and that makes me sick.

I remember going to Smith's office at Holy Ghost parish one day to talk about the marriage. It was dark and filthy and smelled like smoke and beer. Papers were piled on his small, wooden desk, and there was one lamp on the desk for light. It was the middle of the day and it was like I was in a dark cave.

As a non-Catholic wanting to marry a Catholic, I was required to sign a piece of paper that said I would promise to raise any children we had Catholic. I mean, what kind of an organization is that to make a condition of marriage the signing over of your children to them? I signed the paper just to do it. I just wanted to get out of there. I didn't like Smith, and he didn't like me.

I'm done. Here's Larry again:

****

Your child-raping priest married us at Holy Ghost—I call it Holy Spook—Church on Albuquerque's southeast side. I try never to drive past it because when I do I puke.

To this day I have not forgiven myself for letting Smith marry us. I think of myself as a coward and a fool for letting it happen. I've even labeled myself "despicable" for allowing him to marry us.

There's one other thing.

Jean and I and the kids have lived in Albuquerque three different times. It was during the first tour here that I dealt with Smith again. Somehow he knew that I was back in Albuquerque. He called to say that he was dying and was living in a nursing home. He wanted to see me.

I went to see him twice. One of those times he said he needed my forgiveness before he died. "I don't think I'm going to make it to Heaven," he told me.

I did forgive him. He died in 1987.

Someone asked me recently if I believe in Hell. I said I did. Then he asked if I hoped that Smith was there. My response:

"I don't wish that on anyone."

"That's like saying, 'Please forgive me for raping me and beating the shit out of me.' Why was I supposed to return to the organization that raped me?"—Larry Monte Jr.

Eleven

Screwed Again

The most important thing I've learned from being raped by a priest and being essentially crazy for thirty-eight years, and that I will tell others who've gone through the same, is this: Don't go to the Catholic Church for help.

I tried, and it just screwed me up more.

You see, up until I got that first letter from Sheehan on July 19, 2002, I had been going to mass and had been a member of the club. As a kid I often went to mass five days a week. In fact, I never missed Sunday mass—I didn't want to burn in Hell for eternity—until I got that letter from Sheehan. I'm still astounded, disgusted and insulted by it. Basically what he said was that they can't defrock or fire rapist priests because they're part of a special club, the "order of Melchizedek."

I've thought about that a lot since then, probably way too much. But think of it this way. If one of your sons or daughters or nephews or nieces were raped and abused repeatedly over a period of years, would you want the rapist brought to justice?

Would you want the rapist turned over to the cops and prosecutors? Would you want the rapist sent to prison? Would you want the rapist to rot in prison?

I don't think I'm pushing it too far to say, yeah, you would. Who wouldn't?

And, if one of your loved ones, or even a neighbor, was raped, would you expect the kid to go to the rapist for help?

Probably not.

Now think of this: If your child was raped by a guy, who was, say employed by a big corporation or was a member of a prominent social club, would you expect the business or the club to turn him over to the cops?

I'm going to guess again that the answer is yes.

Imagine you wrote to the president of the company or the club and asked him or her to fire the rapist and turn him over to the law. That would be a normal and necessary request on your part. Now imagine getting a letter from the big guy or gal saying something like this:

Dear Fool, Loser and Idiot:

Do you not know by now that we are better, smarter, more highly educated and holier than you are?

Do you actually think we care that you were raped by one of our officers? Do you think we care that you've been in and out of hospitals, gone crazy and that you've suffered the humiliation of being bound up in a straitjacket? Do you think we care that your life and mind have been destroyed by our rapist? Do you think we care that you've tried to kill yourself because of what our guy did to you?

Well, fool, we don't!

We could give two shits about you. You're nobody to us because, one, you're not an officer of our firm or member of our club—thank God!—and, two, we protect our own. They're more important to us than you are, and they always will be.

You see, dummy, our corporation goes back a long, long way, and we're special. The guy who fucked you in the ass, and thousands of others of our officers who have done the same to children, are special people. They're from the Order of Bullshit, which dates back to the beginning of time and our special founder. We can't fire him or kick him out of the club or turn him over to the cops. Once a member of the club, always a member of the club. And club members are better and more important than you are.

Fool, we have our own rules and regulations and we are above the law. No one tells us what to do. We make our own rules and scoff at your civil authority.

We could probably suspend him for a bit and not let him make widgets or wear funny hats for a while. To not make widgets and not wear those funny hats is severe and grave punishment. We've done that with a lot of our rapists, and believe me, they are hurting! There are a lot of people out there—who, by the way, are smarter than you are—who think that our restrictions on our rapists are too severe! We agree, but hell, for PR purposes, we've got to at least make it look like we're doing something.

You have to know that even though you were raped, most of our rapists practiced their Godly art twenty, thirty or forty years ago. What's the problem? Buck up and just get over it, asshole.

Now, what you'll need to do, fool, is apply for membership to our club, or come to work for our company. We've got so many ridiculous rules, traditions, ceremonies, rituals and rites that it would make your head spin. After all, we are the only true company and club. In no other company or club will you find the succession that we have here in the Order of Bullshit. We have a succession all the way back to the original Bullshitter. So screw you.

Now, let me tell you all the wonderful things I have done for the company and club. Naah, won't waste my time with you.

In conclusion, fool, and please, please, get this through that tiny mind of yours:

We're better than you. We answer to no one but ourselves, and we don't care about your pain, suffering, shame, guilt or feelings of worthlessness. You are worthless!

You need us, we don't need you.

Get lost!

Yours in hypocrisy, lies, indifference, arrogance, and Bullshit.

****

That's what Sheehan's letter said to me. It said that I was nothing but fool who didn't understand that rapist priests can't be fired because they're part of a special club that answers to no one: the Order of Melchizedek.

Being treated like a worthless fool is one reason I decided to file a claim against the Archdiocese of Santa Fe in 2007.

But I still didn't understand what was going on.

You see, I never wanted money from you people and your religion. I just wanted some recognition of my worth as a human being, an apology, and action to bring all of your rapists to justice so as to protect other children. I also wanted you to ask me for my forgiveness, which I wanted to give.

I'm actually not some raving lunatic and madman who's consumed with rage. At least I wasn't until I met Smith, your man of God, and until I got that letter from Sheehan.

I believe in the scriptures. You know what scripture is? It's a love letter, a series of them. How many hundreds and hundreds of times is the word "love" used in scripture?

I believe in Christ's teaching to love one another. I believe in doing unto others as you would have them do unto you. I believe in kindness and love. I believe in joy, but up until I started this book, I hadn't had any. I hadn't felt true joy since before I met Smith, and that was thirty-eight years ago.

I didn't want to deal with legalities. I wanted to face you people man-to-man, expecting you creeps to do the manly thing and treat me with dignity and respect. I wanted you to do the manly thing and admit your sins, admit my anguish, and humbly and sincerely ask for my forgiveness.

I wanted you to do as you say and as you teach us to do. I wanted you to practice what you preach. I wanted you to act as Christ would have acted. But you didn't do as Christ did. You left me to rot.

That's all I wanted, and I never got it. Instead, I got a letter and phone calls saying, "No big deal. We can't fire these guys. You don't understand. They're members of our club and our club is holy and sacred and out of the reach of the law."

I wanted to handle this with love. Instead, you gave me lawyers and Canon Law and rules and regulations. I expected you to handle this like men, true men, men imbued with Christ's love, with his compassion, sincerity and humility.

You didn't, though. Instead, you've acted like devils. No one will ever convince me that you're not.

I wanted to handle this like I think Peter would have, with love and with kindness. So, as part of the settlement, I demanded an audience with Sheehan.

I got it. It was in the late spring or early summer of 2007. I drove to his office on Albuquerque's westside on what used to be the University of Albuquerque and what is now the campus of St. Pius High School. You guys call it The Catholic Center.

It was early afternoon, maybe one-thirty or two. I was ushered into Sheehan's office and his conference room. There was a crucifix on the wall and a large, oblong, wooden table. We shook hands upon meeting and sat down in padded chairs of Southwestern design. The room was sparse, it was only Sheehan and me, and we sat across from each other.

From the outset all he did was try to pass blame. I couldn't believe how fast he was to pass the blame. It was the same stuff I had gotten in his letter and the phone calls. This happened a long time ago, he had personally cleaned up the archdiocese and what a great guy he was for doing that. It was all about him and his actions and what he was doing. He wasn't interested in hearing what I had to say.

He had read my deposition, but I could tell that he didn't really understand what had happened to me, or my pain and my sense of betrayal. He was in a position of Godly authority and was not to be questioned, and that was the gist of it.

I asked him about Sharp and Perrault. I wanted to know where they were and why they hadn't been punished and turned over to civil authorities. He didn't want to touch the matter of Sharp, and he said that Perrault had disappeared off the face of the earth, which I found amazing. This was a character that had had several lawsuits filed against him, how could he just disappear off the face of the earth? How can you disappear in today's society? I'll bet that if we were to poke around your palace in Rome we'd run across that child rapist.

I felt as though Sheehan was talking down to me.

The whole thing was amazing to me. When they want to put their authority on something, they do, just like that. When they don't, the disavow it and move on.

I looked into Sheehan's eyes and all I saw was darkness and cold. There was nothing Christlike or loving about him. To me he was just another corporate honcho who cared nothing about me and everything for the corporation.

He did tell me that he was sorry, and he trotted out his old line about how I needed to return to the Church and its "sacraments." He talked about my redemption and said that my redemption had to come from the sacraments.

At that point I felt as denigrated as I have ever felt. He was telling me that in order for me to get redemption, I had to return to the organization that had raped me. That's like somebody being violently raped and having the shit beat out of them going back to the rapist and asking for his forgiveness. That's like saying, "please forgive me for raping me and beating the shit out of me."

Why was I supposed to return and apologize to the organization that raped me? It was sickening and it boggled my mind. It was like he had dropped a steel door between me and the Church. I honestly couldn't register it at all in my mind. When I heard that I was pretty much done with the Catholic Church.

That's when it really hit me. Why, why, why, would I want to return to the religion that raped me? Why was I asking them for help? Why was I seeking peace and joy from them? Why was I so bound to them? Why was I seeking my salvation in them?

I was disgusted with Sheehan and myself. I felt humiliated and shamed all over again. I felt like puking. I didn't, though. I just got angrier and more disgusted as I listened to Sheehan and stared into his cold, dark eyes for those fifteen minutes.

I can't blame Sheehan for Smith having raped me. That began in 1972 when James Peter Davis was archbishop of the diocese. I also concede that Sheehan and the Church in general have adopted strict policies against child sexual abuse. I wish that his attitude toward me and other priest-rape victims represents tone deafness, and not a desire to protect the image of the Church above all else. However, I believe the latter.

Nor do I believe that Sheehan or anyone else can't find Perrault. He's got time. Or he could have it if he stopped writing dumb things for the archdiocese's website. There's a page on the site about Sheehan's bishop's shield. He spends time writing about his bishop's shield.

Here's a tip, Sheehan, on how you should spend your time: Hunt down the rapist who fucked children in your archdiocese.

Sheehan claims as his personal motto, "Love one another constantly."

It would be nice if he and his church actually practiced that. They don't. We're supposed to *love and obey them*.

Sheehan did try to show some love to me, I guess. As it turned out, he had a gift for me—a trinket!

Actually, it was a six-inch-tall pewter crucifix on a wooden base with a pewter ring around it—kind of like a really big halo. He told me that it was his personal gift to me and that he himself had blessed it. He pushed it across the table to me and told me again that I needed to return to the faith and its "sacraments."

All I could think of were those TV evangelists who lay hands on people and personally bless and cure and heal them. You have no idea how cheap and denigrated I felt.

He took the symbol of God's perfect love, and for me, trashed it. He didn't apologize, admit wrong or ask for my forgiveness. He expressed and showed none of God's love.

For me it was like being raped all over again. It was actually worse than the physical acts with Smith. My brain was hurting and throbbing. I cannot describe to you the pain or the humiliation I felt again. I had wanted the truth and love and light and decency, and all I got were lies, darkness, arrogance and evil. What was wrong with me? How could I ever have thought that I would find Christ's love in Sheehan or the Catholic Church? Why did I need them?

Smith had told me hundreds of times that God had sanctioned his raping me. And now, here was an archbishop telling me that I had to return to the church that raped me, that God wanted me back amongst the perverts and rapists. Do you understand my rage and anger? Can you? I know now that God didn't sanction Smith's rapes. And I know now that God doesn't want me back amongst that crowd.

As I said, the meeting lasted fifteen minutes. When I left I was enraged and furious. I was fuming, and I never felt so alone or empty as when I walked out of that office. I knew that the Catholic Church would never be for me again, and I felt like I had lost my best friend.

I wanted to break something and burn myself again and bang my head into a wall. I desperately needed a tool to open my skull. Once again I wanted to take my brain out and scrub it clean. I just wanted the filth, the shame, the guilt and the humiliation to be gone.

I put Sheehan's crucifix on the passenger seat of my white and blue Ford, diesel, 250 four-door pickup truck and drove away.

I left it there for a few days as I stewed and fumed and tried to comprehend why, why, Sheehan wasn't a man and why he and his church had screwed me again.

Then one day I went out to the driveway and the truck. I took Sheehan's trinket off the front seat, walked to the truck's rear end and put the thing underneath one of the rear tires.

Then I got into the cab, started the engine, slammed the truck into reverse and crushed the crucifix.

Then I shut the truck off, got out, picked up the pieces and threw them in the garbage.

Good riddance.

"Don't be afraid to speak."—Mary Claire Monte

Twelve

Don't be Afraid to Speak

Dear Fellow Survivors,

I'm healing, thanks to my wife Jean, our children, friends, Sergeant Pat, my shrink, Dr. Reinhart Schelert, and God.

I'm losing the shame and the guilt and the horror and that intense and overwhelming pain that has been with me for thirty-eight years.

My purpose in writing this book is simple: I had to talk about the rapes to begin healing myself. I've got PTSD and have lived in a constant state of alertness all these years. My body has been pumping out way too much adrenaline and wearing itself out, and my doctors told me that if I didn't deal with this and find some peace and joy, I'd be dead in a few years.

At one point I wanted to die. I wanted this all to end. Now, though, I want to live. And I am.

I want to give back to the Catholic Church all that it gave me. I don't want this garbage any more. Since they gave it to me and since they refuse to fully acknowledge their sins, and since they still harbor child rapists and put the interests of their bureaucracy over those of this world's children, and since they refuse to act with the honor, love and dignity that Christ showed, they deserve all that I and all of you others can throw at them.

I wanted to let anyone else in my position know that you no longer have to hide in the darkness and be afraid of the evil bureaucracy. We have the power; they don't. They can't hurt us anymore. We have to let the world know what they did to us. We can come out of the darkness and into the light and talk about this. We can defeat evil. We no longer have to live with the shame, guilt, pain and sense of worthlessness that the bureaucracy and its rapists gave us. We don't have to keep their evil secrets anymore and be accomplices to their crimes. We can be free.

It has taken me a long time to get here—thirty-eight years to be exact. My pain was so great for so long. So too now is my desire to shout and scream and demand justice.

If my anger and rage and going public like this helps just one person, I've succeeded. All I really want is that when I do die and I'm at the gates hoping for entrance, I hear God say, "Job well done, Larry. Job well done."

Can you imagine that? That's all I want.

I'm a man, and thus I am flawed, and I have asked forgiveness for my shortcomings and sins.

I want those who still follow the bureaucracy's rules to understand what their "shepherds" did to us and what they continue to do to us by blaming the news media for their troubles for daring to report the truth. I want those who sit in those pews to know how I feel when they blindly give the child-rapist-protectors their money, minds and souls. I want them to at least question why they still give their loyalty.

I've asked dozens of Catholics why they go to church. The most frequent answer I get is, "I don't know." My mother still goes to Annunciation—the place that ruined her son's life. We're estranged now because I can't take it that she still goes there. When I asked her why one day, she answered, "It's a different building."

I want people to dig into scripture and the Church's teachings and see how they have taken Christ's simple words, "Love one another," and turned them into a soulless bureaucracy, complete with golden chalices, palaces, expensive vestments, rules for everything, mountains of money and gobs and gobs of real estate. I want them to understand that the Church has taken Christ's words and turned them into a hideous monstrosity and an evil empire that controls people through guilt, shame and the abuse of authority.

But most of all, I want to protect this world's children. I don't ever again want a child hurt like I and others were hurt. If this helps to that end, then I have done well. I want the world to know, and I want the child rapists and their club to pay.

Remember the words in Matthew:

"And whoever welcomes a little child like this in my name welcomes me. But if anyone causes one of these little ones who believe in me to sin, it would be better for him to have a large millstone hung around his neck and to be drowned in the depths of the sea."

****

For thirty-eight years I kept the bureaucracy's secret. That made me an accomplice to its crimes. By refusing to talk about this I hurt myself and my family and friends. I was slowly coming to the realization that I had to talk about my being raped. But it was this poem my thirteen-year-old daughter Mary Claire wrote earlier this year for a class that moved me to finally start cleansing myself of the shame and guilt. Here it is:

Don't be Afraid to Speak

Why does everyone say silence
is golden? In situations I've
encountered, that is not the
case. If you have something to
say, stand up and say it. Don't
be afraid. But my father won't.
He sits in silence,
wallowing in his anguish.
Don't be afraid to speak.

This story isn't mine to tell,
but he won't speak.
He sits in silence.

A truly depressing story—
a nightmare come true.
Don't be afraid to speak.

It scares me, these fits he has.
He has let it consume him, but still
he sits in silence.

Ever since his childhood.
It pains him still.
Don't be afraid to speak.

I don't know what to do
or what to say;
it's not my story to tell.
But still, he sits in silence.
Don't be afraid to speak.

I want to help but don't
know how. Our sainted statues
have paid the price.
It all began with a man, his heart
darker than the blackest black,
and colder than any winter.
And an innocent boy paid
the price. He couldn't tell or
speak. He felt he had to
protect those from his same
fate. He'll take it to the
grave.
He doesn't know how to speak.

Mary Claire, thank you, my dear.
I now know how to speak.

"They consistently failed to take such action and this failure is grounded not in ignorance but in gross negligence."—Fr. Thomas Doyle

Thirteen

Warnings and Lies, Lies and More Lies

Dear Liars and Hypocrites:

Consider these statements:

Santa Fe Archbishop Michael Sheehan: "Our number of perpetrators was high, due in part, to priests who had come to the Archdiocese for treatment from Jemez Springs. While the Paraclete Fathers provided a needed ministry to men who had deviated from their commitment, in all honesty little was known about pedophilia and the best way to treat it. On the advice of psychologists at Jemez Springs, men were often returned to the ministry."—Sheehan letter of Jan. 7, 2004, on the required priest sex abuse audit of his and (all U.S. archdioceses) ordered by U.S. Conference of Catholic Bishops in 2002.

Fr. Gerald Fitzgerald: "As a class, they expect to bounce back like tennis balls onto the court of physical activity. I myself would be inclined to favor laicization for any priest, upon objective evidence, for tampering with the virtue of the young, my argument being, from this point onward the charity to the Mystical Body should take precedence over charity to the individual and when a man has so far fallen away from the purpose of the priesthood the very best that should be offered him is his Mass in the seclusion of a monastery.

"However, in practice, real conversions will be found to be extremely rare. Many bishops believe men are never free from the approximate danger once they have begun. Hence, leaving them on duty or wandering from diocese to diocese is contributing to scandal or at last to the approximate danger of scandal."—Sept. 12, 1952, letter to Bishop Robert J. Dwyer of Reno, Nevada.

Canon Lawyer Fr. Thomas P. Doyle: "When asked about the responsibility to protect young people, Fr. Weber replied:

"'I think the Oblates did what they thought was the necessary thing to correct what was going on, but it wasn't understood in the 80s. I'm going to go back ... to what we understood in the 90s. Because psychiatrists, you lawyers, doctors, FBI, nobody understood what was going on.'

"I have seen this defense numerous times and believe that it is an irrelevant excuse. It matters not whether the Church authorities, in this case the Oblate provincials, knew about the medical/psychological basis for sexual dysfunction or the psychological aspects of the impact of sexual assault on an underage girl. The superiors clearly knew that sex between a cleric and a minor is seriously wrong because it is the subject of a long standing law in the Church's own legal code. They also must have known that sex between an adult male or female and a child between the ages of 14 and 16 is a crime. They had a serious obligation to take corrective action as follow-up to any and all reports of sexual activity by Anthony Gonzales. They consistently failed to take such action and this failure is grounded not in ignorance but in gross negligence.

"Based on my review of thousands of cleric files, I have observed a pattern throughout the ecclesiastical entities in the United States.

This pattern of conduct includes (1) Accepting unfit candidates such as Antonio Gonzales for the priesthood; (2) assigning and reassigning known abusers; (3) failing to investigate allegations according to proper canonical procedure; (4) failing to duly report known criminal behavior to law enforcement authorities; (5) failure to warn the community when transferring a known abuser from one assignment to another; (6) failure to provide even fundamental psychological care to victims; (7) failure to properly document accusations and reports of abuse; (8) failure to isolate accusers; and (9) failure to provide therapeutic intervention in a timely manner for all."—Fr. Thomas P. Doyle, January, 2008, affidavit in the case of Jane Doe vs. Missionary Oblates of Mary Immaculate and Fr. Antonio "Tony" Gonzales (fifteen female victims), 408th Judicial District, Bexar County, Texas. Doyle is a Canon Lawyer, historian and an advocate for priest sexual abuse victims.

Let me say this to Sheehan and all you other liars, rapist protectors and corporate bureaucrats: you're vile, lying, evil pigs.

To keep it short, I'll just say you're pigs. What else can I call those who refuse to turn rapists over to the cops, who send them back out into parishes to prey on and rape more children and then pretend like you didn't know that they could destroy children?

Let's start with Sheehan's twisted and despicable letter.

"While the Paraclete Fathers provided a needed ministry to men who had deviated from their commitment."

Deviated from their commitment? Jesus, archbishop, get it straight, THEY RAPED CHILDREN! THEY RAPED CHILDREN! THEY RAPED CHILDREN!

How many times do you have to be told, you despicable human being you, you apologist for the rapists? There were forty-four raping priests in your archdiocese between 1950 and 2002, as well as two credibly accused deacons.

Seventeen of them, including Smith, were ordained by you guys. Smith had a record prior to being hired by you guys. Remember, he had been kicked out of Christ the King Seminary in New York State for messing with children.

You and your insurers paid $25.3 million in settlements, $4.7 million in attorney fees and $1.1 million for counseling for 193 people. Isn't it telling that you spent nearly five times as much on lawyers than you did on counselors!

The lie of your letter, Sheehan, and the lies of all your other bought-and-paid-for members of the club, is that "little was known about pedophilia and the best way to treat it."

Little was know? Really? Well, let's read some more letters from Fr. Fitzgerald. What a saint that man was. He screamed and shouted about the dangers of child rapists and almost no one in your club listened. He told you repeatedly that your pedos couldn't be cured and that they should never be sent back out to parishes where they could prey on children. You didn't want to hear what he had to say because he was spoiling the party. Your club members didn't want to hear that child rapists couldn't be cured, were vipers and devils and needed to be put on a remote island where they could harm no one but themselves. And you guys kept all this stuff secret.

Here are some more warnings to your club members from the 1950s and 1960s from Father Fitzgerald:

This one was on Sept. 18, 1957, to Archbishop Edwin Byrne of Santa Fe, the man who helped him found the 2,000-acre Paraclete compound in the Jemez Mountains in 1947:

"For the sake of preventing scandal that might endanger the good name of Via Coeli we will not offer hospitality to men who have seduced or attempted to seduce little boys or girls? These men, Your Excellency, are devils and the wrath of God is upon them and if I were a Bishop I would tremble when I failed to report them to Rome for involuntary laicization. It is blasphemous to let them offer the Holy Sacrifice. Experience has taught us these men are too dangerous to the children of the Parish and neighborhood for us to be justified in receiving them here. Your Excellency can if you wish say—you do not wish to interfere with the Rule experience has dictated.

"It is for this class of rattlesnake I have always wished the island retreat—but even an island is too good for these vipers of whom the Gentle Master said—it were better they had not been born—this is an indirect way of saying damned is it not?

"When I see the Holy Father I am going to speak of this class to His Holiness—they should be ipso facto reduced to lay men when they act thus."

That was written in 1957. What is it about vipers, rattlesnakes and devils that you don't get, or that your club members didn't want to get?

How about this one that Bishop Matthew F. Brady of Manchester, New Hampshire, wrote to Fitzgerald regarding one Fr. John T. Sullivan who liked to poke young girls in his archdiocese. Brady was wondering if Fitzgerald would be willing to take the rapist priest and treat him.

"His problem is not drink but a series of scandal-causing escapades with young girls. There is no section of the diocese in which he is not known and no pastor seems willing to accept him. He is at present suspended since July 11, 1956. He is 40 years of age and 15 years ordained.

"At times I have considered him insane, diabolically cunning, and again, as at present, sincerely remorseful. The solution of his problem seems to be a fresh start in some diocese where he is not known."

Three days later, on Sept. 26, 1957—the day I was born—Fitzgerald replied:

"From our long experience with characters of this type, and without passing judgment on the individual, most of these men would be clinically classified as schizophrenic. Their repentance and amendment is superficial and, if not formally at least subconsciously, is motivated by a desire to again be in a position where they can continue their wonted activity. A new diocese means only green pastures.

"We have adopted a definite policy not to recommend to Bishops men of this character, even presuming the sincerity of their conversion. We feel that the protection of our glorious priesthood will demand, in time, the establishment of a uniform code of discipline and of penalties. We are amazed to find how often a man who would be behind bars if he were not a priest is entrusted with the *cura anamarum*. Whereas, a more positive position, such as Your Excellency is taking in this case, would seem to add up to the prevention of these weak and irresponsible men from trailing their unlovely interpretation of the priesthood here and there throughout the country. If the discipline were more uniform and certain, priests before ordination could be instructed and duly warned, and this would be a deterrent to the initiation of these vicious habits.

"To sum up: we are willing to shelter Father with a program that will help him save his own immortal soul. But, should he come to us under these conditions, it should not be with any hope that he will be recommended to another Bishop even after he has spent some months with us. We happen to know quite well the diocese he mentions. And even though it is true that many Bishops, especially in the West, are in need of priests, yet I do not know of any Bishop who would accept a man with his record.

"I trust that this does not seem too severe. But I have my own soul to save, and I do not recommend such men for the *cura animarum.*"

I'm sure that Fitzgerald and Brady saved their souls, but God help the rest of you.

Here's another one. On August 11, 1960, Fitzgerald wrote to respond to an inquiry about a raping priest:

"Father, in God's name, get this man laicized as quickly as possible. This extreme type will never be converted. Men who sin repeatedly with little children certainly fall under the classification of those who 'it were better had they not been born.' He will hurt the church, and he will hurt your community. However, as a layman, the civil authorities will make short work of his activity and place him in the protective custody that his type merit. Otherwise, sooner or later he will kill or be killed. There comes a time when an individual who has repeatedly abused his priesthood should get retributive action.

"As there are many little children in this canyon, where I am the shepherd of souls, I could not in conscience consider receiving him here."

On June 30, 1961, Fitzgerald wrote to Bishop Ernest Primeau, who succeeded Brady in Manchester, New Hampshire, again about Fr. John T. Sullivan:

"He wants activation. And, what is quite disturbing in and similar cases, there seems to be a generic lack of comprehension of the damage done by his past."

In this letter, Fitzgerald went on to talk about your sick and twisted requirement of celibacy. It's funny, you tell us to go out and screw like rabbits without birth control and have kids, kids and more kids, but you won't allow your priests to marry and have sex, which is our most basic human instinct and need. You condemn homosexuality as unnatural, sick and wrong, yet you see nothing unnatural about demanding that men remain celibate and deny their most basic human desire for their entire lives. Fitzgerald continued:

"The main reason why I personally have hesitated to recommend laicization in these cases has been because Mother Church, in Her present discipline, leaves these men in the world but still under the obligation of celibacy. To me, and I think to a great many other priests, it seems like telling a man to go to hell to expect him to observe priestly chastity in the world when he obviously is not capable of observing it. I feel that these men should be laicized, but I do wish that this laicization would leave open for them a plank on which to walk towards salvation, the prospect of the Sacrament of Matrimony. I am in the hopes that this matter will be given serious consideration by the proper committee in the Ecumenical Council."

On Sept. 13, 1961, Fitzgerald wrote again to Bishop Primeau to tell him that he had temporarily let Fr. Sullivan go to a parish in Gallup, New Mexico, to serve. Sullivan was sent there to temporarily replace a sick priest. The Bishop of Gallup had asked for the replacement:

"Under the circumstances there was nothing for me to do except to suggest to Bishop (Bernard) Espelage that he write to Your Excellency and take the matter up with you."

Five days later, Primeau wrote back to Fitzgerald:

"I am most apprehensive about his doing parish work because of his past history. I shall await a letter from Bishop Espelage and will express my fears to him as best I can.

"As you know from previous correspondence, this is not an ordinary case. It is one with a long history and I fear for those entrusted to his care."

Consider this letter that Fitzgerald wrote on May 7, 1963, to Bishop Vincent Hines of Norwich, Connecticut, about one of the bishop's priests in his care:

"I am very much of the opinion that when a padre has fallen into the classification of this young man, he needs a very solid jolt to attempt (if this is possible) to achieve the realization of the gravity of his offence. Personally, I would want to spend the rest of my life on my knees asking God's mercy for I know of no more terrible threat than the words of Our Lord: 'Those who tamper with the innocence of the innocents—it were better if they had never been born.'

"What I am personally afraid of is that these men have the equivalent of that which the Scriptures put in the form: 'I will harden their hearts lest they be converted.' Actually of course we believe the hardness comes out of the heart itself, but I am afraid to let this type of man go immediately back to the altar after having violated the living altar of the human soul."

As you can see, Fitzgerald was usually pretty blunt. But he seemed to pull his punches on August 27, 1963, when he wrote to Pope Paul VI about the priest rapist problem:

"Problem that arise from abnormal homosexual tendencies are going to call for, not only spiritual, but understanding psychiatric counseling. Personally, I am not sanguine of the return of priests to active duty who have been addicted to abnormal practices, especially sins with the young. Where there is indication of incorrigibility, because of the tremendous scandal given, I would most earnestly recommend total laicization."

He wrote to your big guy, your big chief, your great leader about your raping priests and you people did nothing. I'm wrong about that. You did do something. You continued to cover up the problem, support and harbor the rapists and move them around from parish to parish, and you continued to fuck the children. You chose to protect your bureaucracy and your club and its members rather than protecting the world's children. If that isn't the exact opposite of Christ's teachings, I don't know what is. If that isn't pure, unmitigated evil, I don't know what is.

I really don't think that Christ—your founder—would have kept boy-raping priests in the club. I don't think he would have been gentle with them. I think he would have turned them over to the authorities. I'm guessing that he himself would have put millstones around their necks and thrown them into the sea. I don't think he would have tolerated one of his priests saying to a kid, "Fuck me up the ass, God wants you to."

What do you guys think?

On Sept. 10, 1964, Fitzgerald wrote to Bishop Joseph Druick of Nashville, Tennessee, who was in Rome at the Vatican Counsel. In this letter, Father Gerald, as he was called, detailed what he had seen in his years of treating priests at the Paraclete:

"When I was ordained forty-three years ago, homosexuality was a practically unknown rarity. Today it is—in the wake of World War II—rampant among men. And whereas seventeen years ago eight out of ten problems here would represent the alcoholic, now in the last year or so our admission ratio would be approximately 5-2-3: five being alcoholics, two would be what we call the 'heart cases' (natural affection towards women); and three representing aberrations involving homosexuality. More alarming still is that among these of the 3 out of 10 class, 2 out of 3 have been young priests.

"I mention this because it would seem in America at least this type of problem is more devastating to the good standing of the priesthood than anything else. It is very infectious and the prognosis for recovery extremely unfavorable. The majority of psychiatrists, physicians, and experienced priests are not sanguine of permanent recovery. Therefore it would seem that more careful screening—especially the study of family background and personal motivation—is definitely in order.

"Bishop do not quote me because this is given you in strictest confidence, but we know of several seminaries that have been deeply infected and this of course leads to a wide infection."

Fitzgerald's warnings weren't enough for you people. Even bishops who knew about these things and who wanted to do the right thing had trouble doing so. Here's a December 29, 1964, letter of Bishop Primeau telling Bishop Bernard Espelage of Gallup, New Mexico, that he shouldn't hire the raping Fr. John T. Sullivan. Yet he agreed to release Sullivan from his jurisdiction and let the Gallup Bishop hire him:

"Frankly, although we do not plan to take Father Sullivan back into this diocese, I am hesitant to have you assume responsibility for him because of his past record. You are acquainted with this from previous correspondence, so I shall not repeat it. If you wish further information, we shall be pleased to send it to you.

"Should you decide upon incardination (hiring him and assuming responsibility) for Father John T. Sullivan, please let me know and I will prepare the documents of excardination (releasing him from my jurisdiction). This will become effective upon issuance of your decree of incardination."

Let's look at that fine priest of yours, Fr. Sullivan, who died in 1999 after a glorious, thirty-five-year career of raping young women and girls. He was ordained in New Hampshire in 1942. He almost didn't make it into your club. On June 14, 1937, L.P. McDonald, the head of St. Mary's Seminary in Baltimore, Maryland, wrote to Manchester Bishop John B. Peterson saying that he didn't want Sullivan back as a student.

"I regret to have to tell you that the faculty here feels that John T. Sullivan of your diocese ought not to return for his studies for the priesthood. He is practically hopeless in things intellectual. Usually we allow two years before we drop a man for studies, but in this case it would be simply a waste of time and money for him to return. His fundamental education is very weak; he has little natural ability. On the other hand he is a good boy and is deeply religious. But we feel that he could not possibly succeed in Seminary studies."

The "practically hopeless" Sullivan got into a different seminary with the help of his bishop, and he was ordained in 1942. He might have had little natural ability in the way of intellectual matters, but he pretty much got right to work on the sex side of things.

He fathered a child in 1949, but only after arranging a botched abortion for the mother. In 1952, he stalked a nursing student there as well. Between 1953 and 1957 he abused a young woman. It included "fondling, oral sex, digital penetration and partial vaginal penetration," according to the Manchester diocese's 2002 sex abuse audit. "The acts took place in the victim's home, parish rectory, automobile and lake."

Between 1942 and 1944—right after he was ordained—Sullivan messed around with a fifteen-year-old girl. She reported "abuse of kissing, hugging, fondling, sexual intercourse took place in Plaistow, NH. These acts took place in an automobile, the parish rectory and the church," the audit records show.

He was suspended on June 16, 1952, for "improper advances toward young women."

At one point, diocese officials really came down hard on Sullivan. They ordered him to stop driving a car!

"Due to continued indiscretion and abuse on your part, you are hereby directed to dispose of your automobile within ten days. This direction includes the prohibition to hold a car in the name of any other person or to drive the car of another person," Brady wrote to Sullivan.

In August of 1952, Sullivan was reinstated.

At one point, Brady got a hand-written letter from a parishioner detailing some of Sullivan's acts:

"He has been carrying on a clandestine affair with a high school girl for some time. He brings the young girl to the rectory and they are there all afternoon. It is very hard to bring children up in this world and teach them the meaning of being good Catholics without a young curate acting this way."

A July 13, 1956, Manchester Archdiocese report said this about Sullivan:

"Both men have personally seen Father Sullivan parked on a lonely road in the middle of winter at night with another party, presumably a woman, in the car.

"People living near the cemetery have frequently seen Father Sullivan parked in the cemetery in his car with young women at night.

"It is common gossip in the town (Westville, New Hampshire) that Father Sullivan is the father of the child of a young woman who has just returned to town and in whom he is showing considerable interest."

The letter goes on to suggest that Sullivan was stealing money from parish accounts, particularly from the parish raffle account, and forging checks.

Brady had had enough and suspended Sullivan on July 20, 1956.

At that point, Sullivan began writing bishops across the country trying to land a job. He wrote to seventeen in all, and those bishops wrote to Brady asking him about his raping/child-fathering, abortion-procuring priest:

"My conscience will not allow me to recommend him to any bishop and I feel that every inquiring bishop should know some of the circumstances that range from parenthood, through violation of the Mann Act (prohibiting interstate transportation of females for immoral purposes), attempted suicide, and abortion," Brady said in a December 4, 1957, letter to Toledo Bishop George Rehring.

That letter became Brady's stock answer to bishops who asked about Sullivan, and most of those bishops rejected Sullivan.

I suppose that's fine, but Brady and just about everyone else in New Hampshire knew that Sullivan was screwing underage girls! No one ever called the cops!

Fr. Fitzgerald suggested that Sullivan be laicized, but Brady, who could have done it, didn't. Why?

Sullivan was eventually hired on as a priest in Michigan, New Mexico, Minnesota, Texas and Arizona, and he raped girls in every one of those places.

The Grand Rapids diocese in Michigan paid $500,000 in 1994 to three sisters that Sullivan raped when they were girls. He worked there from 1958 through 1960.

In 1979, a thirteen-year-old girl told authorities in Bullhead City, Arizona, that Sullivan had raped her. Sullivan was sixty-two at the time. He was allowed to plead "no contest" in the case and he paid $550 in fees and penalties and was sentenced to 100 hours of community service. Sullivan retired in 1989 and died in 1999.

I'd like to say it's amusing to read garbage from Sheehan about "men who had deviated from their commitment," but I can't. I'm disgusted by it.

Consider this from one of Sullivan's Michigan victims, Fran Heinemann, who told her story to a *Grand Rapids Press* reporter in June of 2002:

"Heinemann said she confronted Sullivan about the abuse of herself and her sisters when she left a note in his prayer book while he was visiting her parents' home, saying she would tell if he didn't stop. He did stop, so the sisters did not pursue charges prior to the lawsuit.

"'He came down the stairs after reading the note and he looked at me with just a murderous look in his eyes,' she said. 'I'm 57 now, but I still remember that look. But he never came back to our house.

"'He was a bad, bad man.'"

I'll take the "murderous look in his eye" over, "men who had deviated from their commitment."

Do you understand why you people make me sick?

There's no hiding

You can't hide from Fr. Fitzgerald's warnings. They were there, and now they're all over the Internet so the world can see. Nor can you hide from the fact that Fr. Fitzgerald believed that pedophile priests couldn't be cured and that he wanted them put on an isolated island. In fact, he actually bought an island. Rather than me telling you, I'll let Fr. Fitzgerald's successor at the Paraclete, Fr. Joseph McNamara, tell you. This is right out of a 1993 affidavit of his:

> Father Fitzgerald thought that such priests— meaning priests attracted to male children, teenagers, or adults—should be completely segregated from society, and consequently wanted a remote "island refuge" far from civilization where a traditional monastery could be established and such men could live and try to save their souls. This was not an idle pipe dream, but was a goal which Father Gerald pursued. In the late 1950s, Father Gerald wrote to a number of bishops, asking if there were an island in their dioceses which would serve this purpose. One bishop, James Davis, then the bishop of San Juan, Puerto Rico, offered the island of Tortola to Servants of the Paraclete. In 1960, two Servants of the Paraclete went to Tortola, but found that it had several thousand inhabitants. Servants of the Paraclete briefly established a parish ministry on Tortola (meaning that the Servants of the Paraclete served as parish priests), but no facility for receiving guest priests was ever established. Servants of the Paraclete left Tortola at the end of 1960.
>
> Later, in the early 1960s, Servants of the Paraclete established a facility on an island named Carriacou in the Diocese of Grenada. Carriacou was also inha-

bited, and although a small facility for receiving guest priests was established there, the retreat on Carriacou did not accept priests with sexual problems.

In 1965, Father Gerald purchased an island in Barbados, near Carriacou, which had an abandoned hotel, damaged by fire, on it. The hotel was entirely removed from civilization. If I recall correctly, the total purchase price was $50,000. A payment of $5,000 earnest money was made, with the promise of a further $28,000 as partial payment to be paid promptly. This was to be Father Gerald's long sought after "island refuge," but it did not come to be. As is described below, Archbishop (James Peter) Davis (Archdiocese of Santa Fe) ordered Father Gerald to sell the island.

Davis was appointed archbishop of Santa Fe in 1964. He took over from Edwin Byrne, who served from 1943 to 1963. Byrne and Fitzgerald were friends, and Byrne is often referred to as the Paraclete cofounder. Byrne let Fitzgerald have a free hand in running the Paraclete.

Fr. Fitzgerald didn't trust psychologists and psychiatrists. He simply believed that child-raping priests could not be cured. He was forced out of the Paraclete by Davis, and thinking began to change. Here's more from McNamara's affidavit:

> The view of the Servants of the Paraclete was that priests with "psychosexual difficulties" should be segregated, preferably on an island. I've read the March 10, 1993, deposition of Dr. John Salazar. Dr. Salazar acknowledges that he advised Servants of the Paraclete that it was not only unnecessary to segregate individuals with "psychosexual difficulties" from others, but that in fact such segregation would be coun-

terproductive to rehabilitation. Although Dr. Salazar suggests in that deposition that he told (us) that what are now called "pedophile priests" should not be sent out to do supply ministry work in parishes, that was the view of the Servants of the Paraclete to begin with.

If only Davis, who was archbishop when I was raped by Smith, had let Fr. Fitzgerald keep that island. Imagine how many children would have been spared being raped.

Fr. Fitzgerald was the one priest you should have listened to, but you didn't. How you have sinned.

"It has been our sad experience that we get excellent recommendations for gentlemen of the cloth who do not deserve them!"—Msgr. James P. Finucan, chancellor of the La Crosse, Wisconsin, diocese. Jan. 6, 1961

Fourteen

It's Rape!

Dear Everyone:

Especially those of you who have never been raped, let alone raped by a religious authority figure and man of God who claimed that God wanted him to rape you, let's get some semantics straight and let's stop calling rape by anyone "sexual abuse."

I hate the phrase, "Priest sexual abuse." It doesn't describe it by a long, long shot. Call it what it really is: Rape of body, spirit, heart and mind.

It's soul murder.

Smith and your raping cult killed my soul and my spirit and my body for thirty-eight years.

I told you before that I live in a constant state of anxiety and alertness. My body pumps out way too much adrenaline and is wearing itself out. If I don't find a way to get through this darkness and into the light and find some peace and some joy, I'll be dead in a few years. I'm only fifty-two.

I haven't been able to cry since that first horrifying day with Smith in that first motel room where he got out his porn and booze and whacked off all over the room.

I've told you about the suicide attempts and the constant mental pain and shame that makes me want to crack open my skull and scrub my brain with a brush. I've told you how every time the Church's leaders deny or minimize this horror and try to make it sound like it was our faults and protect their bureaucracy at all costs, especially at the cost of our mental health, my body rips with pain as if I were an open wound and someone was gleefully throwing salt all over me.

I've burned myself, banged my head into doors and walls, tried hanging myself, flown into rages for no good reason, thrown furniture, broken dishes and been in anguish, pain and mental torture for thirty-eight years.

If I drive by Annunciation or Holy Ghost, I puke.

Writing this book and reading the stuff about those motel rooms sent me into flashbacks, blackouts, dizzy spells and three days of wanting to puke out my guts.

I have felt ashamed, guilty, worthless, angry and like I'm going to explode at any minute. I did explode in 2006 when I had that breakdown and burned my hands and arms with a cigar. I had kept this stuff in for too long and the pain got to me.

It's like if you put a lid on a can full of garbage and close it tight. Well, the garbage will generate methane gas and it'll build and build until the damn thing explodes. That's what I felt like. I finally exploded.

Let's talk about child rape, or, as the shrinks and clinicians and cult members say, child sexual abuse. It includes everything from showing kids porn to touching them on their genitals, putting their hands on one's genitals and penetration of any orifice of a kid's body with a dick, finger or any other object.

I'll add that it also involves being sprayed with cum by a masturbating Catholic priest, and I'll say that it involves being told by a priest that God wants him to fuck you and you him.

It includes having your dick sucked by a Catholic priest as well.

Child rapists are everywhere. They're in every country, culture, race, class and religion.

Child rape statistics can be tricky because it's believed that less than 10 percent of these kinds of cases are reported to the police. I understand that. What kid wants to admit that they've been "sexually abused?"

The National Resource Council estimates that a low of 20-24 percent to a high of 54-62 percent of the U.S. population has been sexually abused. It's estimated that one in four girls in our country are sexually abused before the age of eighteen, and that one in six boys are. Almost 70 percent of all sexual assault cases in this country—including assaults on adults—are perpetrated on children aged seventeen and under. About 30 percent of those who rape and abuse kids are relatives. The vast majority of the offenders are men, but women are perpetrators in nearly 14 percent of abuse cases against boys, and in 6 percent of the cases against girls, according to federal statistics.

Drs. Julia Whealin and Erin Barnett put it this way:

"Sexual abuse can be very confusing for children. A child who is used or manipulated by a trusted adult might learn that the only way for them to be attended to or loved is for them to give something of themselves or give up their dignity. Some children believe the abuse is their fault or that the perpetrator chose them because they must have wanted it or because there is something wrong with them. If the abuser was of the same-sex, children (and parents) might question their sexual orientation and wonder if they are 'gay.'

"Almost every child sexual abuse victim describes the abuse as negative. Most children know it is wrong and experience fear, shock, anger, and disgust. However, a small portion of children might not realize it is wrong, especially if they are very young or have cognitive delays. In addition, some victims might enjoy the attention, closeness, and physical contact, especially if these needs are not met by a primary caregiver. Together, these reactions make the events very confusing for children.

"If childhood sexual abuse is not effectively treated, long-term symptoms may persist into adulthood. These may include: PTSD and/or anxiety; depression and thoughts of suicide; sexual anxiety disorders, including promiscuity; difficulty maintaining appropriate boundaries with others, including enmeshed or avoidant relationships; poor body image and low self-esteem; the use of unhealthy behaviors, such as alcohol abuse, drug abuse, self-mutilation, or binging and purging, to help mask painful emotions related to the abuse."

According to one study, "sexual abuse survivors are at higher risk for mental health and social functioning problems resulting from feelings of powerlessness, guilt, shame, stigmatization and low self-esteem. Powerlessness damages coping skills and reduces ability to protect oneself from further abuse."

The good news is that child rape and sexual abuse appears to be decreasing in the U.S. According to the National Incidence Study of Child Abuse and Neglect, 135,000 child sexual abuse cases were reported to authorities in 2005-2006. That's down from 217,000 in 1993.

As I said before, kids don't like to tell people they've been molested. More than 30 percent of the victims never disclose the experience to anyone. (I'm wondering how they came up with that one, since kids don't tell.)

Nearly 80 percent of the victims initially deny the abuse. Of those who do disclose it, about 75 percent of them do it accidentally.

People who were sexually abused are more likely to commit crimes and abuse themselves.

Nearly 50 percent of the women in our prison systems say that they were sexually abused as children. More than 75 percent of the nation's serial rapists say they were sexually abused as kids.

Seventy to 80 percent of child sexual abuse survivors say they've abused drugs and alcohol. More than 75 percent of teenage prostitutes have been sexually abused as kids.

Kid rapists have multiple victims. Seventy percent of them have between one and nine victims, while at least 20 percent have between 10 and 40 victims. Some serial child molesters might have as many as 400 victims in a lifetime.

We don't know just how many Catholic priests have raped children here in the past 60 years. That's because many—possibly most—of the victims have never come forward.

The John Jay College of Criminal Justice study ordered by the U.S. Conference of Catholic Bishops in 2002 found that 4,392 U.S. priests had been accused of raping kids between 1950 and 2002. That's 4 percent of the 109,694 guys who served as parish priests in the U.S. during those years. The report said that 10,667 survivors had come forward up to that time. The abuse was more than just a handful of wayward bishops and priests. Ninety-five percent of the archdioceses in the U.S. had allegations of priest rape against them, according to the report. Read it:

"Of the 195 dioceses and eparchies that participated in the study, all but seven have reported that allegations of sexual abuse of youths under the age of 18 have been made against at least one priest serving in ecclesiastical ministry in that diocese or eparchy.

"Of the 140 religious communities that submitted surveys, all but 30 reported at least one allegation against a religious priest who was a member of that community."

That means that out of 235 of your little bureaucracies in this country, only 37 didn't report any rapist priests for those 52 years. You must be so proud of that record. And you people have the nerve to say that the news media has blown it out of proportion. You're liars and hypocrites.

Here's more from your study:

"At the time the abuse was alleged to have occurred, 42.3 percent of priests were associate pastors, 25.1 percent were pastors, 10.4 percent were resident priests and 7.2 percent were teachers. Other categories (e.g., chaplain, deacon, and seminary administrator) were under 3 percent each.

"The majority of priests (56 percent) were alleged to have abused one victim, nearly 27 percent were alleged to have abused two or three victims, nearly 14 percent were alleged to have abused four to nine victims and 3.4 percent were alleged to have abused more than 10 victims.

"Priests allegedly committed acts which were classified into more than 20 categories. The most frequent acts allegedly committed were: touching over the victim's clothing (56.2 percent), touching under the victim's clothes (44.9 percent), cleric performing oral sex (26 percent), victim disrobed (25.7 percent), and penile penetration or attempted penile penetration (22.4 percent). Many of the abusers were alleged to have committed multiple types of abuse against individual victims, and relatively few priests committed only the most minor acts.

"The alleged abuse occurred in a variety of locations. The abuse is alleged to have occurred in the following locations: in the priest's home or the parish residence (40.9 percent), in the church (16.3 percent), in the victim's home (12.4 percent), in a vacation house (10.3 percent), in school (10.3 percent), and in a car (9.8 percent). The abuse allegedly occurred in other sites, such as church outings or in a hotel room, in less than 10 percent of the allegations. The most common event or setting in which the abuse occurred was during a social event (20.4 percent), while visiting or working at the priest's home (14.7 percent), and during travel (17.8 percent). Abuse allegedly occurred in other settings, such as during counseling, school hours, and sporting events, in less than 10 percent of the allegations.

"In the 51 percent of cases where information was provided, half of the victims who made allegations of sexual abuse (2,638, or 25.7 percent of all alleged victims) socialized with the priest outside of church. Of those who did socialize with the priests who allegedly abused them, the majority had interactions in the family's home. Other places of socialization included the church, in the residence of the priest, and in various church activities."

So your priests poked kids just about everywhere they could: in churches, schools, in rectories and at sporting and social events. God, you people are sick. And you wonder why the world is in an uproar? It was just open season on children for you guys, wasn't it?

Here's some more:

"To date, the police have been contacted about 1,021 priests with allegations of abuse, or 24 percent of our total. Nearly all of these reports have led to investigations, and 384 instances have led to criminal charges. Of those priests for whom information about dispositions is available, 252 were convicted and at least 100 of those served time in prison. Thus, 6 percent of all priests against whom allegations were made were convicted and about 2 percent received prison sentences to date."

Now I'm betting that in 99 percent of these cases the cops weren't called until after all this was made public. How many times did your people call the cops when they actually got reports of the rapes? Answer that.

I'll answer. Probably none.

The fact is, with the exception of a few of you, your flunkies covered up the rapes and the porn and the fondling and the blow jobs. Here's a January 6, 1961, letter from Msgr. James P. Finucan, chancellor of the La Crosse, Wisconsin, diocese regarding your profligate rapist Fr. John T. Sullivan. He was writing in response to a letter he got from Msgr. Thomas S. Hansberry, chancellor of the Manchester, New

Hampshire, Diocese. In an earlier letter, Hansberry had warned Finucan not to hire Sullivan. First, though, here's part of Hansberry's December 28, 1960, "Confidential" letter to Finucan:

"He (Sullivan) has been in bad odor in this diocese for several years, is suspended and is not permitted to say a public mass in the diocese. The Most Reverend Bishop is not able to recommend him for service in any diocese because of his scandalous actions which have extended over many years. He left New Hampshire a few months ago ostensibly to enter Via Coeli (the Paraclete) on his own initiative and we viewed with alarm the thought of the authorities there to recommend him even for weekend work because of his past history. He is known throughout the state of New Hampshire for his efforts to seduce teenage girls and he left there in the nick of time after his last escapade."

Well, there you go. Sullivan was known throughout the entire state of New Hampshire for poking teenage girls—a crime—and the accessories to his crimes in the Manchester diocese never called the cops on him. And they were relieved that "he left there in the nick of time" after his latest sexual escapade with a girl.

Read Finucan's response to that letter:

"Thank you for your very honest analysis of the problems of Father John T. Sullivan who is now seeking refuge in the Diocese of La Crosse. We cannot tell you how grateful we are for your honesty. It has been our sad experience that we get excellent recommendations for gentlemen of the cloth who do not deserve them!"

It's right there. Your bishops lied about their raping priests.

Yearly amendments to 2004 John Jay report, and new audits now put the number of raping priests at 5,768, which is 5.3 percent of the 109,694 active priests. The number of victims who have come forward to file claims is now up to 15,235.

The problem is most likely much, much bigger. If you take New Hampshire's rate of abusing priests at 8.9 percent of the priests in the state between those years, and multiply it by 2.6 victims each, you get 25,383 victims. Some estimates have put the number of victims between 100,000 and 280,000. One estimate says the number of raping priests might be as high as 9,872.

Consider this: A 1994 survey of 453 pedophiles by the National Institutes of Health found that those child rapists had more than 67,000 victims! That's 148 kids per pedo! Apparently, that's average. Now think of those priests who had absolute authority over kids and easy access to them. And now consider this: You protected them, and your bishops, bureaucrats and cult members reassigned them from archdiocese to archdiocese and from parish to parish so they could, as Fr. Fitzgerald said, find greener pastures and rape more kids.

Say it is 280,000 victims. Know that their mothers and fathers and aunts and uncles and brothers and sisters and wives and husbands and children have suffered in some way because of your rapists. It's a horrifying picture.

Let's consider some more stats. As of July 1, 2010, those ranks of the raping priests include 19 bishops! The list includes 186 brothers, 44 deacons and 17 seminarians. It also includes 75 nuns who have been accused of sexually molesting children.

I know you people deny, deny, deny and deny and say it wasn't much of a problem and that most bishops didn't tolerate raping priests. Read more, liars. A June 12, 2002, study by *The Dallas Morning News* reporters Brooks Egerton and Reese Dunklin found that nearly two thirds of the Church's then-U.S. Bishops had allowed priests accused of sexual abuse to keep working.

The newspaper's investigation found that "at least 111 of the nation's 178 mainstream, or Roman rite, Catholic dioceses are headed by men who have protected accused priests or other church figures, such as brothers in religious orders, candidates for the priesthood, teachers and youth-group workers."

The list of rapist enablers included all eight of the American cardinals at the time.

So screw you when you say it wasn't a big problem and that the news media has blown it out of proportion. That's a lie and you know it.

That list of enablers in 2002 included Sheehan. Here's what the paper wrote about Sheehan:

> "Yet Archbishop Sheehan, as bishop of Lubbock in the 1980s, let at least one accused man keep working in remote parishes for years—which was one reason that the West Texas diocese later had to settle lawsuits too. He has said he sent the Rev. Rodney Howell into treatment for alcoholism in 1986 after a family alleged that the priest had molested two of their children while drunk. 'I think it was true,' the archbishop has said. He returned Father Howell to duty, and the priest worked until he died of cancer in 1993. Before going to Lubbock, Archbishop Sheehan was a high-ranking priest in the Diocese of Dallas. As head of the Holy Trinity Seminary, he admitted Rudy Kos to the school after his predecessor had refused to do so. During the 1997 Kos civil trial, which resulted in the largest clergy-abuse verdict in history, the archbishop acknowledged that he didn't review Mr. Kos's annulment records. They quoted Mr. Kos' ex-wife as saying Mr. Kos 'has some problems' but did not get specific. She testified that she had told an annulment investigator that he was sexually attracted to boys,

brought them to their apartment and never had sex with her. Mr. Kos' two younger brothers testified that seminary officials did little to get information from them about their sibling, who they said had molested them and had spent time in juvenile detention for abusing another younger boy.

So what has happened to all those rapists and enablers?

It's hard to know how many are now dead. But, considering the numbers, not all that many have been laicized, or fired.

According to bishopsaccountability.org, the Vatican has said that between 2001 and 2010, 600 priests accused of sexual abuse had been laicized worldwide. Bishopsaccountability said it had identified 325 U.S. priests who have been laicized.

Posttraumatic Stress Disorder

I've got Posttraumatic Stress Disorder. Was diagnosed at Kaseman Hospital in October 2006 after my sister found me banging my head into that metal door in the alley and burning my hands and arms with a cigar. I had the thrill of waking up in a straitjacket and being injected with as many tranquilizers as the good doctors and nurses could get their hands on.

It's a real illness, not some made-up diagnosis. Combat veterans get it, cops do, so do people who have had terribly frightening and other traumatic experiences. You can get it from watching your mother being beaten up by a drunken old man, from being in a car crash, or any event that truly traumatizes you. It's a lifelong emotional illness that never goes away. Sufferers often re-experience the traumatic events and tend to avoid places, people and other things that remind them of it. I've already told you that I puke if I have to go by Annunciation or Holy Ghost. I don't like the site of crucifixes any more, and, I run for the hills when I see a Catholic priest walking towards me.

PTSD first became a formal diagnose for the shrink world in 1980, but it's been around as long as humans have. In the Civil War, soldiers who got that thousand-yard-stare were said to be suffering from "soldier's heart." In World War I it was referred to as "combat fatigue." In World War II they called it "gross stress reaction." After the Vietnam War, it was called "post Vietnam syndrome." It's also been called "battle fatigue" and "shell shock."

It's estimated that seven to eight percent of the people in the U.S. will get some form of it over their lifetimes. In rape victims and combat veterans, it can be as high as ten to thirty percent. The shrinks estimate that at any given time, five million Americans have some form of it.

One paper by Dr. Roxanne Dryden-Edwards says that "research indicates that people who have been exposed to an extreme stressor sometimes have a smaller hippocampus (a region of the brain that plays a role in memory) than people who have not been exposed to trauma. This is significant in understanding the effects of trauma in general and the impact of PTSD specifically since the hippocampus is part of the brain that is thought to have an important role in developing new memories about life events. Also, whether or not a traumatized person goes on to develop PTSD, they seem to be at risk for higher use of cigarettes, alcohol and marijuana. Untreated PTSD can have devastating, far-reaching consequences for suffers' functioning and relationships, their families and for society."

Some of the symptoms of PTSD are:

Flashbacks and re-experience of the trauma, troublesome memories, recurring nightmares; avoidance of people, places and things to the point of being a phobia; general numbing of emotional responsiveness; chronic signs of hyperarousal. That includes sleep problems, trouble concentrating, irritability, anger, poor concentration, blackouts, increased tendency and reaction to being startled and hypervigilance to threat.

Here's some more:

"The emotional numbing of PTSD may present as a lack of interest in activities that used to be enjoyed (anhedonia), emotional deadness, distancing oneself from people, and/or a sense of a foreshortened future (for example, not being able to think about the future or make future plans, not believing one will live much longer)."

Those are all me. I've got them all. I now avoid Catholic churches, am hypervigiliant, haven't cried since I was fifteen and have experienced no real joy since that Catholic priest plied me with booze, porn, pills and dicked me up the ass.

I'm in counseling now, and I'll let Dr. Reinhart tell you about that.

I've been screwed up for thirty-eight years. For that long, my life has been one long debilitating, life-sapping nightmare.

What a life.

Your priests and you people gave that to me.

You will take it back, and you'll take it back with joy and appreciation, won't you?

No. I'm not asking or pleading with you rapists and power and control freaks anymore. You're taking it back. You're taking all of it back from all of us, and you're taking it back now.

Am I understood?

"It is very difficult to have forgiveness without justice, and when justice is not being done, that can thwart the forgiveness and the healing process. When that happens, the victim is still left holding the bag and doesn't move toward forgiveness."—Dr. Reinhart Schelert

Fifteen

Defective to the Core

Dear All of You Who Don't Understand:

I could keep talking here, but I know that most of you, ah, make that all of you, are dismissing me as an angry nut.

I can hear it now: "Oh that Larry, he's just so angry. So angry. Why doesn't he just get over it?"

You damn straight I'm angry. You would be too if you were raped by a priest in the name of God and then told that priests can't be fired because they belong to a special club that's above the law. You'd be angry if that happened to you, and then it'd be okay to be angry, wouldn't it?

Since my anger might cause you to dismiss what I've been saying, especially about the shame and the guilt and the sense of worthlessness that child sexual abuse victims feel, I'll let my shrink, Dr. Reinhart Schelert, tell you about it. He's been treating sexual abuse victims for twenty years, so you might have a little harder time dismissing him.

So here's the good doctor:

In sexual abuse there is a great deal of shame involved, and it is devastating to the human spirit. Abuse victims' first impulse, and you often see this in rape victims, is to say, "I was bad because I was available."

I treated a woman—she's given me permission to use her story—who was sexually abused at the age of five. When she came to me, she was all sincerity and she said, "You know the reason I was abused? It's because I'm a girl."

She had totally taken ownership of the shame and believed that there was nothing that could be done. That's what sexual abuse victims do; they take ownership of the shame.

Up until thirty years ago, the word "shame" wasn't used in psychological literature. It wasn't used, as John Bradshaw said, because we were ashamed of shame. But shame is simply devastating. People who feel deep shame think to themselves, "I am deeply inadequate. I'm defective. I will never measure up. There is something flawed within me. And if that wasn't the case, I would not have been singled out by that guy and it would not have happened to me and I would not have let it happen to me. I should have done this and I should have done that, and I didn't, and so I'm defective to the core."

When you feel that way about yourself, that you're a slob who's not worth anything more than being a sex object, and that that is the only attention you are going to get in life and that no one is going to believe you anyway, you're stuck. It's a double whammy, and that is why it is so devastating to the human spirit.

In Larry's case you have the shame, and on top of that, sexual abuse by a religious authority. That is now an added layer that is as significant as the shame itself because you have a God representative perpetrating the crime. So the child, in the first place, owns and internalizes the guilt and the shame, primarily the shame more than guilt, and that is destructive to the human spirit.

Larry feels that he is defective to the core and unworthy, both in God's sight and in man's sight. And now he's got this huge piece to deal with of how his mother inadvertently contributed to that because she was so blatantly affirming of priests when he was a child. It was the whole "Priests can do no wrong" thing, and Larry was going to be a priest and so forth and so on. She unwittingly became a co-conspirator.

He feels that he is defective to the core, and his mother hasn't helped that feeling. She keeps telling him to get over it and to stop hassling her and to leave her alone. She's said things like, "It's only because of my prayers to the saints that you have gotten where you are. Why don't you just let go?"

His mother keeps reinforcing the shame when she says, "Priests don't do that sort of thing." The archbishop (Sheehan) is in that sense also an unwitting co-conspirator because he has in effect told Larry, "Well, we can't fire the priests because Church teachings say that priests are priests forever."

You look at that and say, hold on, he's (Sheehan) reinforcing the shame. That doesn't work and that is so destructive to human beings.

Instead of telling Larry that priests are forever, it would have been more helpful if he had said something like, "This has been destructive. It is a terrible shame and guilt on the Church and we've got to get rid of these priests no matter what it costs us, and we're just wrong and please forgive us."

It's really as simple as that. But in so many ways, the Church just can't do that. Their mindset is that the institution is more important than anything else because it is God's only true church, and therefore, "we can't allow Satan to destroy us."

I'm not judging anybody's heart in terms of whether they're bad or evil, God forbid. The Catholic Church hierarchy believes that they are the only true church and that anything that assails it is from evil.

It is important to remember that the Catholic Church acknowledges two sources of authority: biblical authority and Church authority. What happens in practice is that the Church's interpretation of scripture always winds up being superior.

For example, the archbishop's (Sheehan) letter to Larry saying that Church teaching is that a priest is a priest forever. Where are they getting that? It sure seems very self-serving because there isn't an ounce of truth of that in terms of the biblical witness.

The archbishop's letter where he told Larry that priests couldn't be fired and that he needed to return to the Church and its sacraments because it was the only true church just piled more shame and guilt on Larry. It was like saying, "How dare you remove yourself from the source of the only true grace."

So that's what Larry's up against, the mindset of "We can't get rid of these guys even though they're really sick and need a great deal of help and they're not going to stop (abusing)."

It's not my job to bash anybody, but that is what the system does. If they could acknowledge the problem and say they're trying to do well, it would be better for Larry and others in his situation. But there seems to be a blindness that says, "We can't just say that we screwed up and we are sorry and we will make these guys responsible in terms of justice and get them to the authorities."

They talk about forgiveness and mercy, but if you've got a priest who abuses children, you don't give him his job back. A guy who robs your till at the store, you don't give him his job back. Forgiveness doesn't necessarily mean that you give an abusing priest his job back. That's a contradictory message.

The healing process that has worked well for my sexual abuse patients is similar to the grieving process as (Elizabeth)

Kübler Ross first described in 1960: denial, anger, bargaining, depression and acceptance.

Right now (May, 2010), Larry is at the denial stage. His denial is, "I'm bad. I allowed it; it's all me." That's denial coupled with shame.

I am a pastor and therapist. I have a B.A. and Master of Divinity in biblical studies from Abilene Christian University, a Master of Theology in Counseling Psychology from Trinity Evangelical Divinity School, a Dr. of Ministry from Fuller Theological Seminary and served eight years on active duty in the U.S. Navy, and seventeen years in the reserve as a Navy chaplain.

I operate primarily from a family systems perspective and attempt to thoroughly integrate biblical principles into all my professional pastoral counseling. I specialize in individual and family dysfunction, including abuse, trauma, shame, addiction/recovery and 12-step support. I'm trained in crisis intervention, including EMDR (Eye Movement Desensitization and Reprocessing).

I'm trying to get Larry to reflect on the damage the abuse did to him and to get to a level that is more than just an expression of anger, hurt and pain. I want him to go beyond that and to engage his family members as well. That is often left out in the healing journey. It is almost impossible to get to a more fuller and thorough healing without engaging what winds up being conspirators and unwitting co-conspirators.

We talk about what a colleague, David Ausburger at Fuller Seminary, said was "Carefronting," and that is the height of Christian love, or Godly love. It means "in the other person's highest good." It's not good for his mother or sister or for Larry to just fuss about this and for his mother to say, "I didn't know. I didn't know."

It has to be much more in-depth than that, and it has to be a process of engagement. For Larry, it means talking to his mother and saying, "Here is what I have against you," and then going on a journey of forgiveness.

Forgiveness is the big piece of healing that is most misunderstood. It is the most effective tool, and it is the most misunderstood tool.

Forgiveness is misunderstood, and there is a lot of confusion about what it looks like. The popular view is that it means just letting go and the "forgive and forget and don't let it bother you" attitude.

That is not accurate. I've spent a good deal of time trying to understand what authentic, biblical and genuine forgiveness looks like so that people don't succumb to the attitude of making forgiveness a caricature of itself. It is the single most important tool we have, and it is being used inappropriately and poorly.

The Rwandans did it well. They spoke the truth. They held each other accountable, but they said, "We are not going to hold it against you. We are going to start over." That is genuine forgiveness, and if you miss either of those steps, then it doesn't work.

That said, it is very difficult to have forgiveness without justice, and when justice is not being done, that can thwart the forgiveness and the healing process. When that happens, the victim is still left holding the bag and doesn't move toward forgiveness.

My job is to get Larry past his anger and say, "Look, it's not the Church. It is this sick individual and these sick individuals." Because when you don't do that you tend to generalize things. It's sort of like saying, "Well, the government is like this and the government is like that."

That's a system that winds up being self-protective, and in some ways that is understandable. But in terms of healing from the damage, generalizing and blaming the organization won't work. It is misguided and ineffectual. I'm having Larry write in a journal, and I think it is good that he has decided to go public with his story.

In my opinion, people don't like to acknowledge and talk about shame because they don't have an antidote for it. The only antidote to shame is grace. By grace we mean that while we are yet sinners, Christ died for us. We have ultimate value and significance while we are yet sinners, not after we get ourselves cleaned up.

This is a little prejudice of mine, but the Catholic system is a sacramental system that tends to perpetuate guilt and shame, rather than accenting grace. It's the mea culpa of going to the stations of the cross and being told, "You're disgusting, and we are having to shed Jesus' blood again right now in the mass because you are so screwed up," rather than, "He died once for all so that our sins can be forgiven and he loves us enough that while we were yet sinners, he died for us."

A healthy response is to say, "Thank you, Lord. Now I am cleansed and I am holy and I can hold my face up and I am not responsible for killing you every time I go to mass."

I'm trying not to judge, but it does seem that the Catholic system inadvertently perpetuates shame.

In the biblical definition, grace is underserved merit or underserved favor. A person who is filled with shame feels like there is nothing they can do to recreate themselves, that they are defective to the core, and that the only thing they can do is try harder to redeem themselves.

In the sacramental system you are told that someone has died for you and that you must live a life to atone for it. In the grace system, we acknowledge our own inability and our own incompetence and understand that we will never be able to perfectly measure up, and even though we won't, we still have been given the gift of grace.

We just accept that the debt has been paid, that we have been set free, that we have been released and that we are worthwhile and valuable, not because of what we are able to accomplish, but because grace is given to us. It has been given freely to us as a gift.

Our response should be gratitude. In other words, we don't go on living as if it doesn't matter how we live. It is not, "Eat, drink and be merry." It just means that we can never measure up, but we are worthy because of who we are. It means that we are motivated to live a life of dedication and devotion while knowing that at the end of the day we might fall short.

I incorporate these things into my practice. My job is to help people identify and remove those things that block them from receiving God's grace. I'm not the purveyor of grace, I'm just a servant who can scrape away some of the manure that keeps people from saying, "I am worthy."

Now, back to sexual abuse and Larry's case.

There is no worse message to a human being than, "You are just a sexual object to be used, and by the way, God is okay with that because his anointed-one-forever is allowed to do that, and he might get slapped on the hand and moved around, but he is not going to lose his job."

That is horrendous. It is more than merely using somebody. It tells you that as a human being, all you are worth is to be screwed. A person carries that for the rest of his or her life.

In child sexual abuse cases, children are not emotionally mature enough to say, "This guy is screwed up and bad, and I'm being used." They can't conceptualize it or verbalize it. There is just no way. A child's brain is not adequately mentally formed to say, "This is inappropriate and this person has a problem, or mom is yelling at me. She's just frustrated. I won't let it bother me."

No, a child thinks, "I'm a bad kid because mom is yelling at me. I need to stop her from yelling at me. I'm a bad kid."

That's shame. Grace is the only antidote.

"Jeff was a Good Samaritan and a solid human being with a heart of gold. He flew to Houston on his own expense. He took time out of his life and his schedule to help another human being."—Larry Monte Jr.

Sixteen

My Life Saved

Dear Intolerant Freaks:

It's liberating to have a leg and your life saved. It causes you to question all that you have been taught and that you believe, and brings to you a clarity that drives you crazy with frustration. It drives you nutty and makes you want to shout and scream because you finally see the hypocrisy, emptiness and hatred in people and organizations, and you can't understand why others don't see the same thing and why they don't rise up in anger and disgust.

My limb and my life were saved in 2005, and that gave me clarity about your business. It made me see that you don't practice what you preach, that you demand of us things that you don't demand of yourself, and that you're a pack of hypocritical, devious, un-Christlike sleazes. It showed me that you care only about yourselves and your rules and regulations and your power and your authority and your control. You care about those things, and not people and their souls. It made me realize that those you condemn so viciously are those we should embrace.

It was early September 2004 and I was in the cigar shop when it was on Louisiana Boulevard in the small strip mall it had been in since it had opened more than thirty years earlier.

We were putting the final touches on some remodeling and I was on an eight-foot aluminum step-ladder moving some ceiling tiles around and getting them in place.

I was high up on the ladder with my back to a wall when I reached too far to my right and fell backwards. As I fell, my left foot got tied up in the ladder step, and as I crashed to the ground, the bone just above the ankle snapped in two. My left elbow shattered as I hit the floor.

The leg bone had snapped in two, the bone had ripped though my skin and was protruding. Blood was gushing out. My foot was attached to my leg only by the tendon. My left elbow was shattered with a compound fracture and it was twisted behind my back. Even the cops and paramedics who came to the scene got sick at the sight of the pool of blood on the floor and my disfiguration.

If you ever want to know what physical pain is, fall backwards off a ladder and get your leg bone snapped in two.

I was taken to the University of New Mexico Hospital where I had two surgeries to repair my leg. A week later I went back for surgery on the elbow, which needed pins and things. I was in immense pain and was being pumped full of pain killers.

After a few weeks I returned to the hospital because I was in so much pain. X-rays revealed that I needed another, corrective surgery. I had it, and as a result, I got a staph infection. It was gradual. The pain remained intense, I started having high fevers, and my blood pressure was way too elevated. I went to my doctor. The nurse looked at my ankle and said I had to get to the hospital immediately.

There they did some blood tests and discovered that I had what's called a MRSA staph infection and the onset of gangrene. MRSA stands for Methicillin-resistant Sstaphylococcus aureus. That's a staph bacteria that is resistant to antibiotics. It's usually caused by invasive procedures such as surgeries, intravenous tubing or artificial joints. About eighty-five percent of the cases are contracted in hospitals.

The symptoms, according to the Mayo Clinic, "generally start as small red bumps that resemble pimples, boils or spider bites. These can quickly turn into deep, painful abscesses that require surgical draining. Sometimes the bacteria remain confined to the skin. But they can also burrow deep into the body, causing potentially life-threatening infections in bones, joints, surgical wounds, the bloodstream, heart valves and lungs."

That was me. The infectious disease doc put me on a regimen of antibiotics. They put a PICC line up my arm, and for three or four months I was pumping this stuff into my body two to four times a day.

I got better for a while, but then the ankle started getting red and infected and inflamed, and the wound where the surgery had been on my ankle started to open and it started oozing and bleeding, and it just got worse. The drugs were making me weak and sick. I started losing weight, and my health in general started failing.

I had to clean and dress the wound every day. I was laid up and depressed and I was going to the hospital three or four times a week for checkups and more drugs, and it all wasn't working.

A year after the fall and the initial surgery, I was still on the drugs, and the wound was still open and oozing.

At one point Jean was visiting our next-door neighbor, a doctor named Jeff who worked as a researcher for a pharmaceutical company. Somehow Jean mentioned my condition to Jeff and he walked over to the house. He looked at the wound. The skin wasn't closing or healing, and he said something like, "You're not supposed to see your bone. Let me make a few phone calls."

That was either a Friday or a Saturday, I can't remember which. By Sunday, he had me on a plane going to see an infectious doc he knew in Houston at the Texas Medical Center. That was fortuitous to say the least because I couldn't get another infectious disease doc in Albuquerque to see me.

I think it was Jeff who booked the airline flight. He got on the plane with me and accompanied me to Houston. He rented a car there—said he was going to make some business calls. That was BS. He flew down with me because he cared about me.

We got down there and Jeff took me to see Dr. Pablo C. Okhuysen. Doc Pablo looked at the wound, drew a bunch of blood, said I needed immediate intervention and called an orthopedic surgeon. Jeff took me to the orthopedic doc and we scheduled a surgery. Then Doc Pablo got me to a plastic surgeon because they were going to have to pull muscle and skin from other parts of my body to fix that wound.

It was crazy and wonderful. Jeff went with me that first day to Doc Pablo, and he interpreted all the medical stuff for me. I spent a few weeks in Houston, and with the help of all four—Jeff, Pablo, the orthopedic and the plastic surgeon—I healed. The wound is closed, we beat back the MRSA infection, and my foot and leg were saved, possibly my life as well. I can walk again without a leg brace or crutch, although I do now stay away from ladders.

Jeff was a Good Samaritan and a solid human being with a heart of gold. He flew to Houston on his own expense. He took time out of his life and his schedule to help another human being. My health was failing at a pretty rapid rate at the time and Jeff really deserves credit for saving my life. He knew exactly what to do, and because he was in the forefront of drug research, knew what new drugs were available to fight MRSA.

He went above and beyond what you would expect anyone to do. I would never have expected anyone to do what he did. He exhibited such a neighborly, Christ-like behavior toward me. My god, he cared! He not only cared, but he acted on it. He did something to help another human being.

It was a real blessing having this guy as our neighbor.

It's funny how God puts interesting and helpful people in your path.

Jeff is a good, decent, caring, honorable and loving human being. He did for me what you people say we must do for each other, that is, love and help one another. He exhibited Christ-like behavior toward me. You people never have. He was more Christlike than anyone I've ever met in your business. Sheehan never did that. He just told me that the priest sexual abuse horror wasn't his fault and pretty much ordered me to return to your business for redemption.

Yeah, Doc Jeff, my former neighbor, was Christlike.

He's also gay. That's right, he's a homosexual.

And you people hate that.

You condemn homosexuality just like you condemn anything, anyone or any practice you don't like. You drum homosexual priests out of the priesthood, but you protect child-raping priests.

You consider what Jeff does in the privacy of his heart and his home a depravity. Here's a line from your Catholic Answers website:

"The Catholic Church thus teaches: 'Basing itself on sacred scripture, which presents homosexual acts as acts of grave depravity, tradition has always declared that homosexual acts are intrinsically disordered. They are contrary to the natural law. They close the sexual act to the gift of life. They do not proceed from a genuine affective and sexual complementarity. Under no circumstances can they be approved.

"Since sexual desire is subject to a high degree of cognitive conditioning in humans (there is no biological reason why we find certain scents, forms of dress, or forms of underwear sexually stimulating), it would be most unusual if homosexual desires were not subject to a similar degree of cognitive conditioning.

"Homosexual persons are called to chastity. By virtues of self-mastery that teach them inner freedom, at times by the support of disinterested friendship, by prayer and sacramental grace, they can and should gradually and resolutely approach Christian perfection."

You people are such control freaks. Do you really expect anyone to believe that there's "no biological reason why we find certain scents, forms of dress, or forms of underwear sexually stimulating?" Look at a hot babe in a thong and you'll be disavowed of that idiotic statement. You don't need to be a biologist or an anthropologist to know that you people are lunatics.

You know what the "gift of life" means for you people? More members to obey you and to give you money.

You call homosexuals to a life of chastity, but your priests have been raping people and destroying their lives for centuries! Your raping priest Smith used the name of God to rape me! Smith masturbated and cummed all over those motel rooms every chance he got. You knew he raped kids! You sent him to the Paracletes. You didn't condemn him.

If I could scream loud enough for the entire world to hear, and I wished I could, I would scream:

"You liars, hypocrites and sleazes! Stop trying to control everyone's lives by your condemnations! Is a priest fucking a boy up the ass and giving him blow jobs an act of grave depravity and intrinsically disordered? You know it is. You condemn what Jeff does, but you protect child rapists like Smith. You condemn homosexuality, but it's no secret that you have homosexual priests. I have known some of them. You teach, but you don't practice what you teach. You teach it, but you don't live it. You are contradictions upon lies upon abuse. You are evil!"

It is example by which we should live and teach. Jeff gave of himself to save my life.

Jeff is a homosexual. He lives Christ's words. You're a church and you live Satan's words. You preach kindness and love. He lives it.

While I was healing and thinking of Jeff's Christ-like behavior, I got to rethinking your teachings. It made me see what you people really are.

I reject your rules. I reject your controlling authority and your Godless and evil behavior. I reject your protection of child rapists and condemnation of homosexuality.

I will take Jeff and people like him every moment of every day.

He showed me love. You showed me, well, you figure it out.

"If you rape children you will be reassigned, but if you provide sacraments to starved Catholics, you will be excommunicated and laicized. We care much more about man-made canon laws than Jesus' mission to feed the sheep and care for the people."—Fr. Marek Bozek.

Seventeen

Money, Hypocrisy, Authority and Power

Dear Princes of the Church:

You people will never admit what you really are, but your actions show it. You're a bureaucracy. You're about power, authority, control, money and hypocrisy. You people will do anything to protect and keep that power, including behaving in direct contradiction to Christ's teachings. You've sold your souls for power and authority. You've become evil.

In fact, there is no more fertile ground in which evil to thrive than a religious organization. In yours, evil has grown and taken control. It rules you.

I'll pull no punches. In these rapist-priests cases, you've done the opposite of what Christ would have done. You've protected the rapists and the criminals instead of the children. You've cared more for the shepherds than the sheep. You have proudly worshiped at the altar of power, authority, greed, control and rank and privilege. You have engorged yourselves from its cup of deceit, lies, arrogance and selfishness. In doing so, you have become evil.

You're an evil monarchy.

You scare people into believing that your club controls the only way to God, and you scare people with Hell and eternal damnation if they disobey your rules, challenge your authority or don't give you money.

The biggest sin in the Church's eyes is not raping children, but challenging your authority. You hate that, and you're quick to punish anyone who tries it. Let's go back to the July 19, 2002, letter I got from your bureaucrat Michael Sheehan. You remember it. He told me it wasn't easy to laicize, or fire, a priest. I'll quote that letter again:

"You expressed concern that all of the guilty priests have not been laicized or defrocked, but it may be that you don't understand the distinction between restriction and laicization.

"Church teaching is that 'thou are a priest forever according to the order of Melchizedek.' It is very difficult in the universal law of the Catholic Church for forced laicization to take place since ordination is forever."

It's extremely difficult for you people to fire priests who've raped children—you've only done that to a few hundred of your rapists in the U.S.—but it's real easy for you guys to fire a priest who challenges your authority.

I'll go back a little. It was sometime in 2007, I think right after I had that ridiculous meeting with Sheehan, that I called one of your offices in Washington, D.C., and demanded to be excommunicated. I didn't want my name on your rolls anymore. I didn't want anything to do with your filthy, despicable, rapist-protecting club. I no longer wanted to be a member of your organization.

Here's a question. If someone says, "I no longer want to be a member of your organization," what are your options?

A. You could act according to their wish and remove their name from any of your lists and have no further contact with them;

B. You could ridicule them;

C. You could demand money from the person;

D. You could say that removing their name is impossible because once their parents have enrolled them in the club, they are members for life.

The answer I got was D, although the middle two fit your character and your sleazy way of operating. I was told that I could not and would not be excommunicated because that's not how things were done and that I was a member of the organization for life. My name could not be scratched off or deleted from your rolls, wherever they're kept. Whatever my wishes or feelings might be, I was a member for life. My wishes mattered for nothing.

That sounds like the Mob, meaning organized crime. Once you're in the family, you can never get out.

Here's the other thing about you vile, piggish control freaks. I didn't join your club voluntarily. My parents had me baptized into your club and sent me to your schools. I had nothing to do with the decision.

That's how you people work. You hook these poor saps, scare the living shit out of them with guilt, shame and Hell, demand their money under the threat of eternal damnation, and then, if they marry and have kids, you demand, again, under threat, that they make their kids members of the club. Then you pump all of your man-made rules and regulations into the kids, scare them with Hell and mortal sins and tell them that they belong to the only real club on the planet. You hook them, and then their children, and then their children's children, and on and on.

That's how you keep and build membership and make money.

You even tell them they have to pump out kids they can't afford because they'll go to Hell and burn forever if they dare use birth control. It's just a way to get more club members, isn't it?

Maybe this book will finally get me off your rolls. I'm challenging your authority with it. Maybe that'll get you mad enough to take me off. Remember, you've only laicized about 600 rapists priest worldwide, out of the thousands. In the U.S., you've only gotten around to firing 325 of the more than 5,700 who have so far been identified as having raped children. I realize that many have died, but it shows how slowly you move.

In contrast, let's take the story of St. Stanislaus Kostka church in St. Louis, Missouri, and of Fr. Marek Bozek. Let's see how swiftly you move to punish people who challenge your authority.

St. Stan's was founded in 1880 to serve Polish Catholics. A year later, Archbishop Peter Kenrick gave, or deeded, the parish's buildings and assets to a parish corporation that was run by six lay people. Normally, the parishes and their assets are controlled by archdioceses and their bishops. The process was different in the case of St. Stan's and other strongly ethnic-based churches. It was done to help get churches established and, probably, to get more members.

The St. Stan's situation, though, is contrary to current Church law, and my, my, how some of your people are pissed about that.

For more than a hundred and twenty years the situation was fine. The parishioners controlled their church, and all seemed well until 2002 and 2003 when the priest sexual abuse scandals began breaking in Boston and other places on the east coast.

In 2002, St. Louis Archdiocese Bishop Justin Rigali began negotiating with parishioners in an attempt to have the archdiocese assume control of the parish's assets, valued at around $8 million.

Rigali left to become cardinal of Philadelphia, and Raymond L. Burke took over as archbishop in December, 2003. Burke wasted no time in trying to bring those renegade

Polish Catholics under control. He made moves to get control of St. Stan's assets and put them in an archdiocese-managed trust.

Parishioners smelled something foul. Many believed that Burke wanted control of the parish so he could sell it to help his sick club of rapist priests pay off their victims in lawsuit settlements.

They basically told Burke to go to hell and that they would not give control of their parish to the archdiocese. That did not go over well with the archbishop. Oh no. Your man of God acted swiftly. In August 2004, Burke began punishing St. Stan's and its members. He reassigned the parish's priest/administrator and moved the so-called pastoral care of the city's Polish community to another church. Burke removed St. Stan's archdiocesan priests. That meant that the parishioners had to go to another church if they wanted to attend mass and receive communion.

The parishioners fought back and found priests in the area who would come and say mass, often in secret. Then they hired Fr. Marek Bozek, a Polish-born priest who was attached to the nearby Springfield-Cape Girardeau Archdiocese.

Bozek, 35, committed a grave sin, though. He left his diocese without the permission of its bishop, and he went to the aid of common Catholics who weren't part of the Church's privileged ruling class. Bozek said his first mass at St. Stan's on Christmas Eve, 2005. The event drew 2,000 people.

You would think that attendance figures like that would have pleased Burke, a canon lawyer. They didn't. In December of 2005, in anticipation of Bozek's first mass, Burke issued a proclamation saying that the action of St. Stan's lay board in defying him by hiring Bozek, and in Bozek going to their aid, amounted to a "schism," a grave-sounding word that carries the automatic penalty of excommunication.

So, Burke excommunicated Bozek and the six St. Stan's board members for challenging his authority. It gets better, though. Bozek continued to say masses at St. Stan's, which he wasn't supposed to do because he was excommunicated.

Then Bozek really got you people mad. In 2008 he started advocating for the right of priests to marry and for the rights of women and homosexuals to become priests. He even said that Catholics should be tolerant of homosexual relationships. Whooh! That didn't sit well with any of you people.

Burke moved to have Bozek laicized, and in 2009, Pope Benedict agreed and bounced him out of the priesthood. He kicked him out of the priesthood. He fired him. But, but, but, pope, what about "according to the order of Melchizedek?"

Sheehan, where were you to tell the pope about the order of Melchizedek? You should write him now—this very second—and get this thing reversed. "Thou art a priest forever according to the order of Melchizedek." Tell him! Pick up the phone and call him! E-mail him! Sheehan! Tell the pope what you told me. Tell him that a priest is a priest forever. Tell him, you hypocritical asshole, that Bozek is from the order of Melchizedek and can't be fired.

Something tells me that Sheehan would probably go along with this one. Fuck the "according to the order of Melchizedek" when a priest challenges a bishop's authority.

So Bozek is excommunicated and laicized, yet he continues to say mass at St. Stan's, and the parish's board continues to refuse to turn over the Church's assets to the archdiocese.

I haven't met Bozek, but I like him, especially his comments to reporters.

"If you rape children you will be reassigned, but if you provide sacraments to starved Catholics, you will be excommunicated and laicized," he told one reporter. "The recent decision proves we care much more about man-made canon laws, than Jesus' mission to feed the sheep and care for the people."

Go on the Internet and read some of the stories about St. Stan's and the readers' comments. Here's a comment on a December, 2005, story about St. Stan's and Burke's despicable actions:

"Is making oneself subject to the authority of a bishop required for salvation in the Church? Was the death and sacrifice of Jesus Christ freely given for all sinners, or was it surrendered to select men to hold as ransom for temporal power and authority? Was the body and blood of Christ freely given for the remission of sin, or given to select men for power to lord over those they have subjugated?"

Here's another one from the same month:

"Raymond, you know what? The world is round. Just look back and think of all the Catholics that were excommunicated because Catholics had to believe that the world was flat!"

And another:

"It is all about power and money! I am a cradle Catholic and so very proud of what the parishioners are doing in standing up to the crazy, power-hungry, arrogant Archbishop Burke!"

So what happened to the power-mad Burke who could not tolerate a challenge to his authority?

He was promoted!

Yeah, you guys were so impressed with his power-madness that you brought him to the Vatican. He's now prefect of the Supreme Tribunal of the Apostolic Signatura, your guys' highest judicial authority.

Here's another good story. It comes from Ireland and involves Fr. James Chesney, another one of your God-representatives-here-on-earth. Turns out that a fresh investigation by Northern Ireland Secretary Owen Paterson has found that your priest Chesney was a leading figure in the Provisional IRA in the early 1970s. That's the group that was at war with Protestants in the area.

In 1972, three cars blew up in a place called Claudy. Nine people were killed and thirty were injured in the crime, for which the IRA took credit. No one was ever prosecuted for those killings and injuries.

But in August 2010, Patterson said his investigation found that there was collusion between the Catholic Church, the cops and the UK government to protect your godly priest from being arrested and charged in the bombings. The probe found that a deal was hatched to transfer Chesney out of Northern Ireland, which was part of the UK, across the Irish border to County Donegal in the Irish Republic. The transfer put the priest outside of Northern Ireland's legal jurisdiction.

A detective on the case had actually made the request to arrest Chesney in 1972, but the request was denied by a higher-up in the Royal Ulster Constabulary who feared that arresting a priest would inflame the already violent situation in Northern Ireland.

Then-Northern Ireland Secretary William Whitelaw held talks with Cardinal William Conway, who headed the Catholic Church in Ireland at the time. They met after being approached on the matter by an RUC official.

So the priest was transferred and nothing happened to him. The cops never questioned him, and the relatives of those nine dead people, as well as those thirty who were injured, never got any justice. Justice was denied and people got screwed in order to protect your asses. That's so typical of what has gone on throughout the ages. Everybody has deferred to you people and your club.

No more.

I'm not deferring to you. Other victims aren't. The news media isn't. The world is finally seeing you for what you are: a bunch of power-mad, control-freak criminals.

You preach justice and love and responsibility, but you don't practice it.

You preach justice and love, yet you persecute people. You excommunicate a priest for saying mass for people who hired him and for challenging your authority.

You hate those challenges, don't you? And it takes you a long, long time to admit you're wrong, doesn't it?

It took 359 years for you people to admit your reprehensible treatment of Galileo the astronomer in the 1600s. His sin? Challenging your teachings and your authority.

You guys taught that the earth was the center of the universe. Galileo discovered just the opposite. He found that the earth orbited the sun. You guys couldn't stomach that, so you convicted him in 1633 of being a heretic. You imprisoned him in his home until he died in 1642 at the age of seventy-seven.

It wasn't until the early 1990s that Pope John Paul II ordered an investigation into the matter and declared that your club had wronged and persecuted Galileo.

How about Purgatory? It's another thing you guys made up. You really solidified it in the 1200s as your dogma. I suppose you could consider the idea a "gift" to people who die in sin. It gives them the chance to still get to Heaven and be with God. But you screwed that one up too. Your people started selling indulgences to the place, that is, time off from Purgatory, and a way to fast-track relatives into Heaven. They used the fear of eternal damnation and the joy of redemption to make money. For a long time, you let them.

You still sell masses for the dead. That's right, you make people pay to have your guys pray over their dead loved ones. What good does that do? They're dead! Their souls are already gone.

When my dad died in 2007 I was even angrier at you people than I am now. The priest wanted money to say a mass for him. I wanted no part of it, but others in the family did, and they bought a mass. I felt betrayed by them. This was the club whose member raped me, whose members raped tens of thousands of kids in the U.S., and who say they can't turn the criminals over to the law. This was the club that treated me like I was worthless, and they wanted a mass for Dad's corpse.

The idea of it made me puke.

They got their mass, and for me, it was just another form of rape.

The club member who was going to say the mass said I couldn't get up and talk, couldn't eulogize my father. Read that again: Your club member told me that I couldn't get up and talk about my father at his funeral.

That was his job, the priest said.

That was my father, the man who raised and did his best to protect me, the man who, when he found out that I had been raped by a priest, tried to help me, the man who did help me.

But now, I wasn't supposed to get up and spend two measly minutes saying nice things about my father, the man I loved, and the man who loved me. He was the man who bought me shoes and food and clothes and put a roof over my head and who taught me so many good things, the man who hugged me supported me and who cried for me when I was hurting. He was my father, and I wasn't to say anything about him at his funeral mass.

Tell me that's not sick. Do you still not understand why I'm angry and why I hate you people? You're so in love with your authority and control that you told a man's son that he couldn't publicly, with a few words, wish his father farewell and love.

Why would I, or anyone else, want a priest—who probably barely knew your dead loved one—to eulogize them? The whole idea makes me sick.

I bolted up out of that pew at my dad's funeral and I gave a short talk about him. You should have seen the hateful look that priest gave me.

****

This has all been a journey of discovery for me. The more I've read and researched your organization, the more I've come to realize that you're just a club, a club me and my teenage buddies could have made up to control and stick it to people and get their money.

Think of it. We could have sat down one afternoon and come up with something like:

"Let's form a club and tell people that we're the only true and real club in the neighborhood, and that if they don't come to our clubhouse every week and give us money, bad and horrible things will happen to them.

"We'll make up our own laws and say that those laws will trump any civil law or authority. Oh, and get this, we'll tell them that the one thing that will make them truly happy, the one thing that will bring them joy and salvation by the truckloads, is to give us money on a regular basis. We'll call it tithing! We'll say that if they don't give us money they'll feel bad! And instead of being nice to them, we'll threaten and berate them every chance we get. We'll tell them that if they've got friends, they can't be friends with the friends unless the friends join our club and give us money.

"If they continue be friends with non-club members, we'll berate them, threaten them with expulsion and say they're going to burn to death. We'll just scare the living shit out of them!

"We can take a little piece of bread—it'll have to be a precise shape and have a precise amount of garlic in it, though—say some goofy words over it and say that it has undergone transmogrification and turned into our founder's body. We'll do the same with beer and say it's turned into his blood. It can't be any beer, though. It'll have to be brewed to exacting specifications and have a high alcohol content.

They'll only be able to drink the beer from bottles lined with gold. If they do otherwise, they burn. If they question us and ask how garlic bread and beer can turn into a guy's body and blood, we'll give them three hundred pages of incomprehensible explanation about it, and then, if they still question us, we'll berate them and threaten them with burning.

"We'll demand that they obey every law and regulation we come up with. If they don't, they burn. Fire scares the hell out of people—always has—and we'll use it as a club over them. We'll tell them to do exactly what we say, but get this; we won't practice what we preach! We'll do just the opposite! If they dare to call us hypocrites, we'll expel them and threaten them with burning.

"We'll set up our own management structure, and the managers will be more important than regular club members. We'll treat 'commoners' as foolish, ignorant children and convince them that they are exactly that. We'll set ourselves up as their leaders, their shepherds, and they as pathetic, lost, ignorant sheep.

"If those commoners break our rules, we'll punish them. If our managers do, we'll protect them.

"All our management decisions will be made in secret, and commoners will have no right to know how we operate. We'll take their money and their property, but we'll put out no financial statements—that's none of their business.

"We'll set ourselves up as the supreme authority on everything. We'll say that when it comes to club matters, our president can't ever make a mistake, that he's infallible! No one with half a working brain cell would believe it, but our commoners won't be able to think for themselves because we'll discourage it by threatening independent thought with expulsion and burning!

"We'll control every aspect of their lives. We'll dictate who they can be friends with, who they can date, who they can marry, how many kids they can have, when and how and with whom they can have sex; what books, magazines, and websites they can and can't read or view; what clothes they can and can't wear; how much money they should give us every month and where they can and can't be buried. We'll come up with some goofy teachings, maybe something like the earth is a large cantaloupe, and if anyone challenges it, they burn!

"Our main mission is to grow the club so we get more members and more money. We'll do that by threatening everyone with burning if they don't join us. We'll berate every other club as inferior, worthless and full of ignorant losers who will burn!

"We'll tell them that they have to recruit other members to our club—that that is their main mission.

"Our reasons for existing are simple: to exercise control, power and authority over people and to get their money so we can live lavish and privileged lives.

"We'll tell our members that poverty and humility are a blessing and they should practice it with unmitigated zeal. But we'll deck ourselves out in lavish, expensive vestments and house ourselves in big, gilded palaces. And, get this: We'll never let those commoners into our palaces. The hell with them! It's none of their business how we spend their money on ourselves.

"We'll make up rules—something like they can eat only turnips on Fridays—that they'll have to abide by under punishment of burning, and then, every four hundred or five hundred years, we'll issue proclamations saying those rules were wrong. And then we'll make up new rules. We'll keep them confused, bewildered and ignorant.

"Our internal and secret motto will be: Make Stuff Up!

"We'll start out sort of legit. We'll say we're about goodness and community service and the commoners and stuff like that, and we'll have rules saying that, but over the course of time, we'll just make it all about ourselves: by the management, of the management and for the management!

"Remember, Make Stuff Up!

"Guys, this is going to be a blast!"

That's what your club sounds like to me: a bunch of childish drunks getting together to form a club to control people.

You've done most of what I've said here. You made up Purgatory and then used the indulgences to it to raise money for churches and roads and bridges. Good god, what frauds!

How about Limbo? You made that up too. You concocted that one in the 13th century as a place where unbaptized infants were sent. They went there as opposed to going straight to Heaven to be with God because, as another one of your rules says, they're born—we all are—with original sin! An infant hasn't done anything except gurgle and spit up a lot. But you freaks can't send them straight to Heaven. No, they have to go through one of your ceremonies and rituals. And you had to exercise control over cavemen and indigenous babies and any other kids who were born in the centuries before you club was formed. You had to figure out a way to snatch their souls, didn't you?

You made up degrees of sin: original sin, venial sin and mortal sin. Mortal sin is mortal, meaning, if you die with one of those on your soul you go straight to Hell. That's bad, the worst thing that can happen to you. Guess what constitutes a mortal sin to you control freaks? Not going to your clubhouse on Sundays! Me and my drunken buddies would have made up something like that. If you don't come to our clubhouse every week you will burn!

So, for more than seven hundred years, all those unbaptized babies, according to your rules, went to Limbo, and I'm sure that many of their parents were heartbroken because of it.

What about babies whose parents didn't belong to your club, didn't believe in it, didn't want to believe or join, or didn't even know it existed? Did they go to Limbo? Does your club want to control every life on the planet?

The answer is obvious. But, you also teach that God gave all of us free will. Free will means that people don't have to believe what you teach or join your club. But you people say that by exercising our free will to not believe you is a sin that's punishable by—you got it, burning!

So in 2007, after more than seven hundred years, you basically junked Limbo. But even then you weren't clear about what you were doing. Here's a passage from the document, "The Hope of Salvation for Infants Who Die Without Being Baptized" that was issued by your International Theological Commission:

> Our conclusion is that the many factors that we have considered above give serious theological and liturgical grounds for hope that unbaptized infants who die will be saved and enjoy the beatific vision. We emphasize that these are reasons for prayerful hope, rather than grounds for sure knowledge. There is much that simply has not been revealed to us. We live by faith and hope in the God of mercy and love who has been revealed to us in Christ, and the Spirit moves us to pray in constant thankfulness and joy. What has been revealed to us is that the ordinary way of salvation is by the sacrament of baptism. None of the above considerations should be taken as qualifying the necessity of baptism or justifying delay in administering the sacrament. Rather, as we want to reaffirm in conclusion, they provide strong grounds for hope that God will save infants when we have not been able to do for them what we would have wished

to do, namely, to baptize them into the faith and life
of the Church.

That's pretty clear, ain't it?

So you made up Limbo and then did away with it.

Then there's the thing about not eating meat on Fridays. I
have no idea how many thousands of years you held people
to that one, but, apparently, you changed that too so that eating meat in Fridays is no longer a sin punishable by burning.

What happened to all those people who went to Hell for
eating meat on Fridays?

I heard one story of a little girl. When the rule was
changed, she asked her teacher, a nun, if all the people who
were in Hell for having eaten meat on Fridays would be let
out now. The answer?

The girl was sent to the principal's office for punishment.
Yeah, she dared question you people.

Let's look at chalices. You've got rules regarding chalices.
They have to be gilded on the inside. A gold chalice for a
priest who's taken a vow of poverty? I'll bet you've spent
more time pondering the metallic composition of chalices
than you have getting rid of rapist priests.

And Celiac Disease. That's a condition where people get
sick if they eat wheat or wheat-based products. Your rules say
that your hosts must be made of wheat. Where has that left
Catholics with Celiac Disease? Out of luck if they've wanted
communion. Well, you just started loosening those rules a
few years ago and now approve some low-gluten wafers. As
of the mid-1990s, you were recommending that men with
Celiac Disease not be priests. You would accept child rapists
into the priesthood, but not some poor guy with a genetic
disease that made him sick if he ate wheat. You've lightened
that up somewhat as well, but it sure takes you people a long
time to show some compassion.

And then there's the infallibility of the pope. That's a good one. It means that when it comes to Church doctrine, the pope can't be wrong because he got his information from God.

The whole idea first developed in the Middle Ages. In 1057, Pope Gregory VII listed twenty-seven statements of papal infallibility in something called the *Dictatus Papae*. One of them said, "the Roman Church has never erred, nor will it err to all eternity, the Scripture bearing witness."

How's that for a self-serving, power-mad statement?

The idea that the pope could say or do nothing wrong when it came to Church matters was codified as Church dogma, as they say, at the First Vatican Council in 1870. Here's what it says:

> We teach and define that it is a dogma divinely revealed that the Roman Pontiff when he speaks *ex cathedra*, that is when in discharge of the office of Pastor and doctor of all Christians, by virtue of his supreme Apostolic authority, he defines a doctrine regarding faith or morals to be held by the universal Church, by the Divine assistance promised to him in Blessed Peter, is possessed of that infallibility with which the Divine Redeemer willed that his Church should be endowed in defining doctrine regarding faith or morals and that therefore such definitions of the Roman Pontiff are of themselves and not from the consent of the Church irreformable.
>
> So then, should anyone, which God forbid, have the temerity to reject this definition of ours, let him be anathema.

Whew! How's that for an unrepentant power grab and arrogance? Now the popester is speaking infallibly for all Christians! You people don't stop. And how about that threat at the end? "Should anyone, which God forbid, have the temerity to reject this definition of ours, let him be anathma."

The dictionary defines anathema as "a curse; a person or thing consigned to damnation or destruction; a formal ecclesiastical curse; and a person or thing detested or loathed."

Well, I guess a lot of American Catholics are cursed and loathed by you people. So are those in Austria, Ecuador, France, Ireland, Italy, Japan, Peru, Spain and Switzerland, because in a massive survey conducted between 1998 and 1992, 36.9 percent of them said they didn't believe that idiotic, self-serving, power-grabbing doctrine.

Now, I know that popes rarely speak "*ex cathedra*," but hell, when they do, we who don't buy that infallibility crap will have to put a string of garlic bulbs around our necks because you people will curse us! You're a "religious" organization that curses people who choose to not believe you. You people are sick.

Curses!

Well, God forbid, I have the temerity to reject that definition of yours.

You people are anathema to me.

Eighteen

Rape through the Centuries: The Church's Sexual Abuse History

Dear Apologists:

The truth can be brutal. That's why we so often shun it. We prefer clinical terms like molestation and sexual abuse instead of the details of what those things really constitute. Same thing with murder and rape. We hide from the details because details shock and appall us. We prefer to live in ignorance and apathy instead of knowing the brutal truth because the truth can shake our beliefs and tell us we've been wrong or ignorant or naïve or unthinking or unquestioning. When you're unthinking and unquestioning you can wind up being a slave to those who seek to manipulate and control you. Who wants to admit to having been wrong and having been an unthinking, and unquestioning dupe?

For forty years or so I was one of the Catholic bureaucracy's millions of unthinking, unquestioning and submissive dupes. I believed and unquestioningly *obeyed* them. And I feared them. It's exactly what they demanded from me and everyone else: unquestioning obedience.

I was more than a dupe. My fear, obedience and my silence made me an accessory to their crimes and cover-ups. I kept their filthy and evil secret.

It was Sheehan's 2002 letter that sickened me and got me reading and thinking about the Church, and it got me questioning as well. In one respect, I should thank him because that letter sent me on a journey of exploration, thought and questioning. I am no longer that unthinking, unquestioning dupe. I am no longer the Catholic Church's slave.

I've told you what being raped by a priest really involves and what it really does to a human being. You know the horror and terror of it; the degradation, pain, humiliation and anger and self-loathing and how it ruins lives forever.

What most of you don't know is that your bureaucracy and its members have been raping boys and girls and men and women and spreading the sorrow and horror of ruined lives and shattered minds for centuries.

Now you can read their history of rape and abuse and cover-ups and secrecy and lies. It comes, not from me, but from Fr. Thomas P. Doyle. He's a canon lawyer, historian, and, since 1984, an unwavering advocate for priest sexual abuse victims. Doyle is a Dominican who was ordained in 1970. From the fall of 1981 through 1986 he served as secretary and Canon Lawyer on the staff of the Vatican Embassy in Washington, D.C. During that time he reviewed sexual abuse complaints against priests. His major involvement in priest sexual abuse cases began in June 1984 with the case of Fr. Gilbert Gauthe in Louisiana, and it hasn't stopped.

Here's part of Fr. Doyle's January, 2008 affidavit in the case of Jane Doe vs. Missionary Oblates of Mary Immaculate and Fr. Antonio "Tony" Gonzales (fifteen female victims), 408th Judicial District, Bexar County, Texas:

13. The Catholic Church was officially recognized as the state religion by Emperor Constantine in the early

4th century. With this recognition the religious leaders, soon to be known as the "clergy," gradually evolved into a separate, privileged class, the most exalted members of which were the bishops. Although celibacy did not become a universally mandated state for clerics of the western Church until the 12th century (2nd Lateran Council, 1139), various church leaders began to advocate it by the 4th century. The earliest recorded church legislation is from the council of Elvira (Spain, 306 AD). Half of the canons passed dealt with sexual behavior of one kind or another and included penalties assessed for clerics who committed adultery or fornication or who had sex with minors. Though it did not make specific mention of homosexual activities by the clergy, this early Council reflected the church's official attitude toward same-sex relationships: men who had sex with young boys were deprived of communion even on their deathbed.[1]

14. Other gatherings of bishops throughout the Christian world, which encompassed what is now Western Europe, Northern Africa, the Middle East and the British Isles, passed laws attempting to stamp out clerical concubinage, clerical fornication and homosexual activity with minor boys.

15. The Catholic Church is organized in geographic regions known as dioceses, from a Greek word meaning a "group." The term was common from the 4th century. The head of a diocese has traditionally been a bishop. Early church legislation was passed by individual bishops for their own territory but the more important legislation with lasting historical impact was that passed by groups of bishops who gathered at

periodic meetings known as councils or synods which were generally named after the place where they occurred. Laws were passed throughout the Christian world forbidding illicit sexual activity by the clergy. These laws, whether the product of individual bishops or groups, did not need the approval of the papacy.

16. By the 9th century collections of the growing mass of legislation began to appear. These were unofficial and generally poorly organized attempts at putting at least some of the known legislation in the same place. Several of the more prominent and complete collections have survived as essential sources for the study of the development not only of church law but of the Christian life in general. The first truly systematic collection was produced by the monk Gratian in 1140. Known as the Concordance of Discordant Canons or more commonly as Gratian's Decree, it consisted of a wide spectrum of texts arranged in a dialectic method with Gratian's own opinions added. Though never officially approved, Gratian's decree became the most important resource for the history of Canon Law. Following the medieval period, the major legislative sources were the popes themselves and the general or ecumenical councils, the most recent of which was Vatican II (1962-65).

17. The practice of individual confession of sins to a priest started in the Irish monasteries in the late sixth century. With individual confession came the Penitential Books, another valuable source for church history. These were unofficial manuals drawn up by various monks to assist in their private counseling with penitents in confession. These books listed the various and sundry acts which the church considered sinful

and provided guidance on the acceptable penance to be imposed. The Penitentials provide a vivid glimpse into the darker side of Christian life at the time. Though it is not known exactly how many such books were written, the more prominent ones have been preserved, studied and translated.

18. Several of the Penitentials refer to sexual crimes committed by clerics against young boys and girls. The Penitential of Bede (England, 8th century) advises that clerics who committed sodomy with young boys be given increasingly severe penances commensurate with their rank, the higher ranking (bishops) receiving harsher penalties. The regularity with which mention is made of clergy sex crimes shows that the problem was not isolated, was known in the community and was treated more severely than similar acts committed by lay men. The Penitential Books were in use from the mid 6th century to the mid 12th century.[2]

19. The most dramatic and explicit condemnation of forbidden clergy sexual activity was the Book of Gomorrah of St. Peter Damian, completed in 1051.[3] The author had been a Benedictine monk and was appointed archbishop and later cardinal by the reigning pope. Peter Damian was also a dedicated Church reformer who lived in a society wherein clerical decadence was not only widespread and publicly known, but generally accepted as the norm.[4] His work, the circumstances that prompted it and the reaction of the reigning pope (Leo IX) are a prophetic reflection of the contemporary situation.

20. Peter Damian begins by singling out superiors who, prompted by excessive and misplaced piety, failed to exclude sodomites (chap. 2). He asserts that those given to "unclean acts" not be ordained or, if they are already ordained, be dismissed from Holy Orders (chap. 3). He holds special contempt for those who defile men or boys who come to them for confession (chap. 6). Likewise he condemns clerics who administer the sacrament of penance (confession) to their victims (chap. 7). The author also provides a refutation of the canonical sources used by offending clerics to justify their proclivities (chap. 11, 12). He also provides chapters which assess the damage done to the church by offending clerics (chap. 19, 20, 21). His final chapter is an appeal to the reigning pope (Leo IX) to take action.

21. The pope's response, included in the cited edition, is an example of inaction similar to that of contemporary church leaders. Pope Leo praised Peter Damian and verified the truth of his findings and recommendations. Yet he considerably softened the reformer's urging that decisive action be taken to root offenders from the ranks of the clergy. The pope decided to exclude only those who had offended repeatedly and over a long period of time. Although Peter Damian had paid significant attention to the impact of the offending clerics on their victims, the Pope made no mention of this but focused only on the sinfulness of the clerics and their need to repent.[5]

22. The repeated violations of clerical celibacy were amply documented in the canonical collections of the medieval period. The most authoritative source is the Decree of Gratian already mentioned. Though man-

datory celibacy had been decreed by the 2nd Lateran Council in 1139, this law was received with neither universal acceptance nor obedience. Medieval scholars attest that clerical concubinage was commonplace. Adultery, casual sex with unmarried women and homosexual relationships were rampant. Gratian devoted entire sections to disciplinary legislation which attempted to curb all of these vices. He demanded that the punishment for sexual transgressions be more severe for clerics than for lay men. His treatment of same-sex activities was less extensive than that of other celibacy violations, yet his attitude is evident because he cited the ancient Roman law opinion that stuprum pueri, the sexual violation of young boys, be punished by death.[6]

23. From the 4th century to the end of the medieval period it is clear that violations of clerical celibacy were commonplace, expected by the laity and highly resistant to official disciplinary attempts to curb and eliminate them. Referring to concubinage for example, one noted scholar said:

From the repeated strictures against clerical incontinence by provincial synods of the twelfth and thirteenth centuries, one may surmise that celibacy remained a remote and only defectively realized ideal in the Latin West. In England, particularly in the north, concubinage continued to be customary; it was frequent in France, Spain and Norway.[7]

24. Clerical sodomy continued to be a known problem though it did not attract as much legislative attention as clerical concubinage, quite possibly because of the ongoing attempts to eliminate clergy marriages. The 4th Lateran Council (1215) repeated the previous

council's condemnation of celibacy violations. It added, however, a specific mention of homosexual sex by clerics and decreed that those found guilty of this transgression were either to be dismissed from the clerical state or confined to a monastery for life. The former amounted to social exile and the latter to imprisonment.[8]

25. The documentation from the medieval period indicates that although homosexual liaisons were not uncommon among the secular or diocesan clergy, most celibacy violations involved heterosexual forms of abuse. Illicit sexual activity by monks was another matter. Although concubinage and even illicit marriages occurred among the monks, the fact that they took vows of chastity precluding marriage and lived a common life theoretically isolated from women meant that their sexual outlets would be considerably restricted. The monks became known for the frequency of homosexual activity especially with young boys. Many monasteries passed local regulations in attempts to curb the rampant abuses. In his Rule, Benedict commanded that no two monks were to sleep in the same bed. Night lights were to be kept burning and the monks were to sleep clothed. Many monasteries enacted their own rules forbidding various kinds of sexual behavior and added punishments that were often more severe than those meted out to the secular clerics.[9] So common was clerical same-sex activity that some scholars have concluded that homosexual relationships were commonly associated with the clergy.[10]

26. There are two aspects of the ecclesiastical legislation and overall attitude toward clerical sexual activity

that stand in marked contrast to the contemporary period. The first is the documented fact that in addition to a stringent admonition by Peter Damian in the Book of Gomorrah, at least two general or ecumenical councils took direct aim at church leaders who supported errant clerics by their failure to take decisive action.[11] The 4th Lateran Council (1215) and the Council of Basle (1449) both recognized the fact that curbing the vices depended on cooperative superiors. The canon from the Lateran Council is succinct:

Prelates who dare support such in their iniquities, especially in view of money or other temporal advantages, shall be subject to a like punishment.[12]

27. The other unique feature of this period is the collaboration of the church with secular authorities in the enforcement of ecclesiastical laws. The Catholic Church was the only Christian denomination and the dominant social force in the medieval period. Separation of church and state was unheard of, which meant that the boundaries between secular and religious were often blurred. Church authorities considered celibacy violations to be more than a purely religious matter. They caused some degree of scandal and therefore were a matter of public interest. To enhance the opprobrium, the church often tried accused clerics in the ecclesiastical tribunals and then turned them over to secular authorities for additional prosecution and punishment. Penalties were harsh and sometimes included execution.[13]

28. No prior reform movement in the Catholic Church had an impact equal the 16th century Protestant Reformation. The reformers were concerned

about a number of problems they saw with the Catholic Church, sexual abuses among them:

The sexual habits of the Roman Catholic clergy, according to reformers, were a sewer of iniquity, a scandal to the laity, and a threat of damnation to the clergy themselves. 14]

29. In spite of attempts to propagate revisionist versions of the Reformation, the Church's primary reaction, the ecumenical Council of Trent (1545-1563), was itself proof of the deeply entrenched and wide-ranging corruption in the Church. Secular princes had urged a reforming council but the popes resisted until 1545 when Pope Paul II summoned one to be held in the Italian city of Trento.[15] The council met in 25 sessions with several periods of adjournment. It ended in 1563 after session 25 when most of the major reforms were enacted.

30. The reaffirmation of clerical celibacy did not conclude without strong opposition from a significant number of bishops who argued that mandatory celibacy was simply not working and accomplished no more than denying priests' "wives" and children a share in their estates.[16] A canon was proposed which would have permitted marriage for clergy but this was rejected and mandatory celibacy re-enforced. The canon upholding celibacy was followed by one which extolled it as superior to marriage:

If anyone says that the married state excels the state of virginity or celibacy, and that it is better and happier to be united in matrimony than to remain in virginity or celibacy, let him be anathema. [17]

31. In spite of the reforming legislation and the establishment of mandatory seminary training, education and formation for priests, the bishops at Trent were no more successful at curbing celibacy violations than their predecessors. Illicit sex with women, men and young boys continued but for a time were much less obvious. By 1566, in the first year of his pontificate, Pope Pius V (1566-72) recognized a need to publicly attack clerical sodomy. The constitution Romani Pontifices promulgated legislation against a variety of actions and practices, including the "crime against nature." This short canon condemned all who committed this crime and prescribed that they be handed over to secular authorities for punishment. Clerics, however, were to be first degraded, presumably by an ecclesiastical court, and then handed over to secular authorities. [18]

32. Two years later the same pope apparently found it necessary to issue another condemnation of clerical sodomy. The constitution Horrendum specifically named clerics who committed "the sin against nature which incurred God's wrath" ("quae contra naturam est, propter quam ira Dei venit in filios diffidentiae.") and stipulated that they be punished with deprivation of income, suspension from all offices and dignities and in some cases, degradation. [19]

33. Summarizing the medieval period, it is clear that the bishops were not as preoccupied with secrecy as they are today. Clergy sexual abuse of all kinds was apparently well known by the public, the clergy and secular law enforcement authorities. There was a constant stream of disciplinary legislation from the church but none of it was successful in changing

clergy behavior. In spite of a millennium of failure, the popes and bishops never gave serious thought to the viability of mandatory celibacy. The variety of spiritual punishments was joined, in the later period, with severe corporal penalties, inflicted by secular authorities. Finally, and most important, at certain periods, church authorities recognized that the problem was not only dysfunctional clerics, but irresponsible leadership.

SOLICITATION IN THE CONFESSIONAL

34. Individual confession of sins by a Catholic to a priest began in the 6th century. Annual confession became mandatory with the Council of Trent. Also, the spirituality of the time prompted many people to go to confession regularly. For some this meant weekly or even daily. By the 17th century the papacy recognized that some priests were using the sacrament of Penance, commonly known as confession, as a way to solicit sex from penitents. The Pope and various regional bishops issued a series of disciplinary laws against solicitation, beginning in 1561 and extending to 2001. Papal laws were promulgated in 1561, 1622, 1741, 1917, 1922, 1962, 1983 and 2001.

35. In addition to the legislation itself, the church courts prosecuted individual cases in great numbers. The most complete records have been found in the Spanish and Mexican tribunals and reveal a shockingly high volume of complaints from women and men, accusing priests of solicitation and sexual abuse in a variety of forms. The most complete study of cases from the Spanish tribunals revealed that between 1723 and 1820, 3775 cases were completed and sen-

tences handed down. The author concluded that this number represents a small portion of the actual cases in that it reflects only those completed and not the total number started and later abandoned. [20]

36. Clergy sexual abuse has been enshrouded in a culture of deep secrecy since the mid-nineteenth century and possibly earlier. It appears that the obligation of secrecy concerning clergy sexual abuse cases was imposed by Pope Pius IX in 1866. The official document that imposes the secrecy was published on February 20, 1866, by the Sacred Congregation of the Holy Office in the form of an "Instruction." This instruction provided clarification on certain aspects of the previous papal constitution dealing with solicitation in the confessional, Sacramentum Poenitentiae (1741) of Pope Benedict XIV. The actual text is as follows:

Par.14. In handling these cases, either by Apostolic commission or the appropriate ruling of the Bishops, the greatest care and vigilance must be exercised so that these procedures, inasmuch as they pertain to [matters of] faith, are to be completed in absolute secrecy, and after they have been settled and given over to sentencing, are to be completely suppressed by perpetual silence. All the ecclesiastic ministers of the curia [court], and whoever else is summoned to the proceedings, including counsels for the defense, must submit oaths of maintaining secrecy, and even the Bishops themselves and any of the local Ordinaries are obligated to keep the secret. [21]

37. After the promulgation of the Code of Canon Law in 1917, the Vatican issued special legislation in 1922 on procedures to be followed in solicitation

cases. This document was sent to the world's bishops but otherwise retained in total secrecy. Unlike previous special legislation aimed at curbing solicitation for sex in the confessional which was public, this document was never publicly promulgated. It contained procedures to be followed in the prosecution of cases of solicitation for sex by a cleric. In issuing the document, the Vatican stipulated that it was to remain strictly confidential. It was not to be openly published or commented upon. No explicit reason was given for this unusual secrecy nor is any justification given for the document or some of the surprising changes contained therein.

38. The 1922 procedural norms, sent by the Vatican to every bishop in the world, introduced several significant elements, including an exceptional degree of confidentiality imposed on the document itself and the persons involved in processing cases. Compared to previous papal documentation confronting clergy sexual abuse, this document contains several significant changes which reveal the church's policy on clergy sexual crimes. Though circulated to all bishops in the world, the document has been retained with a high degree of secrecy since its promulgation.

a. Jurisdiction: Local ordinaries (bishops and heads of religious orders) have the right to process cases included in this document. However, they retain the option of sending such cases to the Vatican's Congregation of the Holy Office for prosecution.

b. Secrecy-officials: Tribunal and other church personnel who are involved in processing cases are obliged to maintain total and perpetual secrecy and are bound by the church's highest degree of confidentiality, known as the Secret of the Holy Office. Those who violate this secrecy are automatically excommunicated and the absolution or lifting of this excommunication is reserved to the pope himself.

c. Secrecy-parties and witnesses: Even the accuser and witnesses are obliged to take the oath of secrecy. The penalty of automatic excommunication is not attached to the violation of the oath. However the official conducting the prosecution can, in individual cases, threaten accusers and witnesses with automatic excommunication for breaking the secret.

d. Anonymous denunciations. Anonymous accusations are not automatically ruled out though they are generally to be rejected. They are to be considered and acted upon if circumstances require and if there appears to be some semblance of veracity to the accusation.

e. Other sex crimes. Title V of the document specifically included homosexual acts between clerics and members of their own sex, bestiality and sexual acts of any kind with children. The document uses the Latin word "impuberibus," which means "before the age of reason." This is defined in canon 88 as one who is seven or under. The Code also contains a canon prohibiting sex with minors which is defined in canon law as one sixteen or under. A careful reading of the relevant paragraphs of the 1962 document (par. 71-73) leads to some confusion as to whom the crimes apply to. It is clear that sex with children is included and sex with males of any age, as well as sex with animals. The only category of possible victims that is unclear is sex with young girls.

39. In 1962 Pope John XXIII approved the publication of renewed special procedural norms for processing solicitation cases. Like the 1922 document, this document was buried in the deepest secrecy. Although it was promulgated in the ordinary manner and then printed and distributed by the Vatican press, it was never publicized in the official Vatican legal bulletin, the Acta Apostolicae Sedis.[22] The document was sent to all bishops in the world as well as to the superiors of religious orders of men.

40. The other sex crimes included under Title V are not crimes connected with solicitation but the actual sexual abuse itself. These are to be processed in the same manner as crimes of solicitation. Thus, the three classes of clergy sexual abuse were cloaked in the highest degree of secrecy. Little was known about either the 1922 or 1962 documents until reference to the 1962 document, commonly known by its Latin name Crimen sollicitationis, was included in a 2001 Letter sent to all bishops from the Congregation for the Doctrine of the Faith on more grave crimes reserved for consideration to that same Vatican office. [23]

41. The 1962 document was issued prior to the promulgation of the revised Code of Canon law in 1983 and therefore would, under ordinary circumstances, have lost its legal force. The recent letter however clearly indicates that it had been in force until May of 2001.

42. The 1922 and 1962 documents are significant because they reflect the institutional church's urgent

desire to maintain the highest degree of secrecy and strictest degree of security about sexual crimes perpetrated by clerics.

43. The public exposure of clergy sexual abuse of youth which began in the mid-eighties was misrepresented by some and mistakenly believed by many to be a new phenomenon which of course it is not. In spite of a series of high profile cases from around the world, the Vatican issued no disciplinary documents until 2001. Although the Pope John Paul II had made eleven public statements about clergy sexual abuse between 1993 and 2004, this was the first attempt by the Vatican to take concrete steps to contain the problem. The document, which is a set of special procedural norms, is not exclusively about sex abuse although that is the predominant theme. It is about the processing of certain crimes considered by the Vatican authorities to be so serious that prosecution of them is reserved to the Vatican itself.

44. The 2001 document reflects much that is found in the 1962 procedural norms. There are significant developments however:

a. The bishop or other superior is obliged to send the results of the preliminary investigation of an allegation of sexual abuse to the Vatican congregation. The officials there decide if the case will be processed in the Vatican or returned to the local diocese for prosecution.

b. The canonical age of a minor was raised from 16 to 18.

c. The statute of limitations was extended to 10 years. In the case of sexual abuse of a minor, this time begins to run from the victim's 18th birthday.

d. All officials involved in processing cases must be priests.

e. Files of cases completed on the local levels are to be sent to the Vatican for retention.

f. The Pontifical Secret, formerly known as the Secret of the Holy Office, is imposed on all officials connected to any cases. No mention is made of imposing the secret on accusers or witnesses.

There is no mention of reporting such cases to civil authorities.

45. Clergy sexual abuse was unknown by the vast majority of Catholics and the general public until a series of revelations took place beginning in 1984 in the United States and in 1988 in Newfoundland in Canada.[24] The culture of secrecy was enabled by the official policy of the Vatican which imposed the highest degree of confidentiality on processing cases of clergy sexual abuse.

46. The Contemporary Era. In our contemporary era popes and bishops have been aware of clergy sexual abuse even though the general public has not been aware of this dimension of church life. The revelation of 1984 in the U.S., 1988 in Canada and later 2002 in the U.S. marked the public awareness of a problem Church officials had been aware of for decades. Although the first public cases were in the United

States and soon after in Canada, it is erroneous to assume that this is a North American problem or a problem restricted to English-speaking countries. Child and adolescent sexual abuse is a problem that crosses ethnic and cultural boundaries. A major difference is not in the existence of the problem but in the manner with which different cultures respond to it.

47. In 1946 Fr. Gerald Fitzgerald, a U.S. priest, founded a small religious community known as the Servants of the Paraclete. The community was started in the archdiocese of Santa Fe, New Mexico and in time had treatment facilities in a number of States and in several foreign countries. The mission of the community was to provide assistance to troubled priests with addiction problems, psychological problems and psycho-sexual problems. From the very beginning the Paraclete Fathers were confronted with clergy who had sexually abused young people. Fr. Gerald believed that such men could neither be cured nor controlled and therefore should not be allowed to function as priests. He argued that they should be laicized, even against their will, as this would be for the benefit of the church community. He made his thoughts known in letters to various bishops as well as in reports to the Vatican.

****

There's more, but that's the heart of it. So, you can see, Catholic priests have been raping people for centuries. You have no excuses now.

"As a result, we are no longer to be children, tossed here and there by waves, and carried about by every wind of doctrine, by the trickery of men, by craftiness in deceitful scheming."—Ephesians, 4:14

Nineteen

Apathy and Moral Bankruptcy Look Behind the Curtain

Dear True Believers:

I'll start here by quoting one of Fr. Thomas Doyle's papers on the priest sex abuse scandal that has rocked the bureaucracy you continue to support:

"The shrinking of the institution and the demand for constant accountability has been hampered by widespread apathy and denial among the general Catholic population. The failure of the laity as a group to rise up in outrage at the knowledge of clergy sexual abuse of the Church's most vulnerable is a pathetic testament to the quality of Catholic moral teaching.

"Far too many are still afraid to think outside of the stultifying ecclesiastical box. Too many more believe the erroneous propaganda dispensed by the institutional Church simply because a bishop or archbishop said it. This is magical thinking at its most destructive level."

I'll go beyond that. It's the mentality of a slave; the mentality of people so mentally and morally lazy that they believe everything they're told; it's the mentality of people who prefer being told what to do and how to think instead of thinking for themselves; it's the mentality of people who apparently would applaud a fiend who raped their son or daughter or niece or nephew or husband or wife, or, who raped God.

Read Matthew 25:40:

"In as much as ye have done it to one of the least of these my brethren, ye have done it unto me."

First, I used to be one of those Catholics who believed everything the priests, bishops, archbishops, cardinals and the pope said. I believed them when they said that priests were better and holier than the rest of us and that we needed them to get to God. I believed that priests were the successors to the apostles and that they could do no wrong. Because I believed so blindly, I was fucked up the ass by a Catholic priest and I let him give me blow jobs and I let him spew his vile sperm all over my fifteen-year-old body.

When that was happening, I believed that Smith was God's representative and that he was, in effect, being inspired by God. Part of me believed that I had to obey him and submit to his sickness. Never again.

Second, are not we all brothers and sisters in Christ? Are not we all members of the Catholic Community? Are not we all brother and sister Catholics?

I would guess that you believe we are. Then why don't you care that I and probably hundreds of thousands of others like me were raped by your priests? By not caring about me and us, by sitting there sheepishly, obediently and mentally, morally and spiritually lobotomized in those pews, you are acquiescing to the rapes, to the harboring of criminals and to the offering of your sons and daughters and nieces and nephews and husbands and wives to be raped as well.

If we're all family, why do you not care that one of your family members was hideously raped for two years? Why do you not care that one of your family members has suffered daily for thirty-eight years with the pain, the sorrow, the anguish, the shame, the humiliation, and the torment of having been raped, degraded and dehumanized by a self-proclaimed man of God? Why do you not care that because one of your family was raped by a priest he tried to hang himself, banged his head into doors and walls, burned his arms and hands with a cigar, caused his wife and his children pain, torment and anguish and sorrow, and got tied into a straitjacket and put into a mental ward where they gave him coloring books and crayons to play with?

Why do you not care that the organization that raped me has refused to turn the rapists over to the law? Why do you continue to give your money, allegiance, minds, spirits, presence and souls to a company that protects criminals?

It's because you're slaves—mental, spiritual and physical slaves—and you either don't know it, or you prefer it that way because it's easier than thinking on your own and getting to the truth. So many people prefer to be led than to lead, or to think for themselves. The ugly truth about humans is that many prefer slavery to freedom because it's easier. It's difficult to make choices, isn't it? It's hard work to research and to educate yourself so you can make informed and moral choices. It's hard, risky and often painful work to take a stance, challenge authority and battle for the truth.

Your company—and that's what it is, a business that's a facilities and risk-management organization that's in the business of selling redemption—has made you slaves. Tom Doyle is right, "the failure of the laity as a group to rise up in outrage at the knowledge of clergy sexual abuse of the Church's most vulnerable is a pathetic testament to the quality of Catholic moral teaching."

The organization teaches, preaches, encourages, fosters and demands obedience, shame, fear, guilt, ignorance, reverence and monetary support. Add those together and you get slavery.

Maybe you're afraid to confront the business' officers for fear of—who knows what. I know that many of you are afraid. I know that many of you really have no idea why you go to church. I said it earlier, the response I get when I ask many of you why you go to church is "I don't know."

God gave you a brain with which to study, think and discern. Use it. To not use it is immoral. Christ used his. He railed against money changers in the temples, hypocrites, heretics and those who used religion to control and use people for personal or institutional gain. Yeah, Christ got pissed, and he got pissed a lot.

Think of it this way. What if a large company, say a big-box retailer, acted the way the Church has acted? What if you went into a big-box, or any retail store, and when you did, its employees pulled down their pants and flashed you? Or say, when you went there with your children, one of the employees snatched your child and took him or her off to a back room and raped them?

Would you be pissed then? Would you be angry? Would you demand that management call the cops? Would *you* call the cops? I'm suspecting you would call the police. What if when you did, the store's management refused to turn the rapist over to the law because they believe their employees are a protected class of humans who are better than you and who are above the law?

What if it became known that more than five percent of the company's employees were child rapists? Would you keep going to that store, buying its products, giving it your money and adding to its profits?

I'm not stretching things here by saying you wouldn't keep going to the store and giving it your business. If it became known that more than five percent of a major American corporation's employees were child rapists there'd be screams and howls and marches and protests and boycotts and investigations and indictments and outrage and condemnation, and that corporation would quickly be out of business.

What makes the Catholic, or any church, different? It's because the Catholic Church has taught and conditioned you to be unthinking, docile, unchallenging slaves. Why do you suspend your thinking and your anger when it comes to the Church and to religion? That's the one place, the most important place, really, where you should apply all your thoughtful energy. After all, it's your spirit and your soul that's at stake.

Do you really think that God wants you to be an unthinking dupe and slave? I don't think he does.

Remember Matthew: "In as much as ye have done it to the least of one of these my brethren, ye have done it to me."

For way too long I wondered why God had abandoned me. Why he had abandoned me in those motel rooms with the cum-spewing Smith? Why he had abandoned me to the Catholic Church's mean-spirited, power-mad, cold and evil arrogance? Why he had abandoned me to the soulless Mr. Sheehan, the man whose only response to me was that the rape of children by priests in Albuquerque and Santa Fe hadn't happened on his watch and that I had to return to the organization and its sacraments?

Then one day—I don't remember when it was—I read Matthew again and it became clear: God was with me in those rooms. I was the least of his brethren, and a Catholic priest raped me. "In as much as ye have done it to the least of one of these my brethren, ye have done it to me."

In raping me, the least of one of God's brethren, a fifteen-year-old, Smith was raping God.

God was with me in those rooms with Smith, and, well, he got fucked up the ass like I did.

Matthew inspired me to speak out against the evil, raping bureaucracy. I will not go to my grave without continuing to speak out for myself and for those who can't speak for themselves because they're ashamed or afraid.

And you, my dear believing, unquestioning, slaving brethren, by refusing to hold the Church accountable for raping me and all those others, you've refused to hold them accountable for raping God. By failing to demand that they turn the people who raped us over to civil authorities, you are failing to demand that they turn over to the cops the people who raped God. By giving your allegiance, obedience, presence, spirit, mind, soul and money to the organization whose members raped all of us, you are giving those to the organization whose members raped God.

"In as much as ye have done it to one of the least of one of these my brethren, ye have done it to me."

Do you understand what that means?

Can you read it? Can you hear it? Can you comprehend it? Can you bust out of your slave chains and take action on it?

You are accomplices to the Catholic Church's rape of God. Will you continue to let the Catholic Church rape God?

Think of the damage done by the child-raping priests and of all those kids-turned-adults who didn't make it in life. Think of, as Tom Doyle calls it, the "toxic swamp" created by the Catholic Church and its raping priests and its officers who have protected the rapists throughout the years.

What about the guys who are in prison because of this? What about the guys who committed suicide? What about the guy on the street who's an alcoholic, drug addict and homeless because of this? What about the shattered minds, the divorces, and the kids who were damaged because their dads were screwed up by this? What about all those children who've been tossed into the sludge pit of humanity because of the Catholic Church and its raping priests?

Do you care about those people? You should. They are your brothers and your sisters. At the least, they're your fellow human beings. Do you care nothing for them? Do you care nothing for the least of our brethren? Do you care nothing for God?

If you think that all of this priests-raping-children stuff is no big deal because the percentages of rapists are small, that it's something that happened in the past, that it's something hyped by the news media in order to embarrass the Church, or that I and all of us should just get over it; if you think that raping God is no big deal, then I have a suggestion for you:

Become an officer of the Catholic Church. You'll fit right in.

****

Anyone with even half a working brain cell can figure this stuff out and see for themselves that the rapist-priests story is a big deal that has ruined hundreds of thousands and millions of lives over the centuries. That's not to mention all the people who have died in name of God through crusades and wars and attempts by priests and missionaries to convert everyone. Your good Catholics came to the Southwest in the 1600s and tortured and killed Indians who didn't care to believe what your priests tried to impose on them. They did the same in the Northeast and the South. If people didn't believe or buy into what they did, they just killed them.

It's really not funny to torture and kill people who don't want to buy into your brand of religion. It's certainly not Christlike.

All this rapist-priests stuff is not made up. The evidence of the accusations, of the cover-ups, of the winks and the nods, and of the constantly transferring the pigs from parish to parish come from the organization's own archives.

I'm not trying with this book to slay a dragon for the hell of it, or to grind an axe just because I want to. The evidence and the horror of this are irrefutable. It comes from Church archives. If after reading this, and hopefully, other books on this sickening subject, you don't rise up out of those pews and demand an end to this, then nothing will change your mind.

If you want to live under the auspices of this dark cloud of sin and injustice, you are entitled to do that. But you are not entitled to support an organization that harbors and comforts child rapists. You have a responsibility to humanity to demand justice for those who have committed crimes and for those who have raped children.

I used to understand your apathy because I used to be you. I'd go to mass every Sunday, listen to the priest and think that was it, and that that was all I needed to know. I too was an unquestioning and unthinking dupe and slave.

But being raped and being locked in psych ward can shake you pretty quickly out of such passivity. It wasn't just that, though. I'd like to think that I've always been spiritual. I began reading scripture at an early age, and I, well, believe. To me, our spirituality is the core of who we are as humans. You can build bridges or tall buildings or great dams or be a great tailor or seamstress, but those accomplishments mean nothing when it comes to spirituality.

That's why I ask all of you to think about this. We are getting ready to walk into eternity. We have been given this time to grow spiritually. Why would we want to dismiss it and be so trite about it? Faith and spirituality are such a critical part of life. Are we going to sit there and be spoon fed without questioning things?

There are so many sources out there documenting this priests-raping-children horror show. We all have the ability to discern the truth. We're compelled to find the truth. You're not going to find it through thirty-five Hail Marys and forty-five Our Fathers and having some guy tell you every Sunday how things are.

God gave you a mind. Use it.

****

Many of my friends and family members are angry that I've left the Church. I tell them why, and they don't understand. They say, "just get over it."

As I told you before, I can't get over it. Because I believed in everything the Church taught and preached, I was raped. Because I believed, obeyed and revered priests as Godly men, I was raped.

I can't just get over it and I can't go back because my eyes and my mind have been opened and cleared. The Church, I now see, is strictly a business, a business and a bureaucracy that sells redemption. It sells redemption by fostering fear, shame, guilt and obedience.

I've read scripture, and nowhere in it can I find where Jesus said, "Go out and start a large bureaucracy to tell people what to do and to take their money."

I believe that were Christ here today and he multiplied those loaves and fishes to feed the thousands, the pope and bishops and cardinals would demand that he charge those hungry masses for the food.

Why wouldn't they? They require people to pay for everything else. They charge you to marry you, they try charging you to sit in mass on Sundays, and they charge you for a mass when you want to say goodbye to a dead loved one.

I came to realize that the Church was a facilities-and-risk-management organization that peddles redemption when I had that visit with Sheehan in 2007.

I was at the archdiocese's headquarters here in Albuquerque and was walking down the hallway to Sheehan's office. I saw nameplates on the doors. One was for the chief information officer, one for the office of accounting, and another for risk management or something. I don't remember seeing anything that actually had to do with spirituality. It would have been nice to see one for the Office of Love or of The Golden Rule or of Kindness or of, and I like these, Office of Doing the Right Thing and Treating People With Dignity and Respect, and Office of the Truth.

There were no such offices.

I remember thinking to myself as I walked down that hall, "Wow. This is a business. It's all about managing revenue and providing these facilities. This is an administrative, risk-management business."

Sheehan claims as his motto, "Love one another always."

He didn't love me. He treated me as a pest and an intrusion into his business activities. I'm in business—started and run my own businesses—and part of me understands why he treated me that way.

Business is not in business to love one another always. Business does not have a heart, business does not have a soul, and business does not seek out love. Business is a cold-hearted thing that seeks profit. It can't have a heart and a soul, because if it did, it would not be able to turn a profit.

The Catholic Church is a business. It has no heart and it has no soul. It's there to manage facilities, turn a profit and manage all the wealth it has accumulated. That's what struck me when I walked down that hallway that day. I thought, "Oh my god, I get it now."

They try to deceive everyone. They put up this beautiful front, but they get people through their most vulnerable places, through their hearts and their souls. Then they say, "We've got them now. We've sucked them in and we're going to get their money. We're going get more money and acquire more wealth."

The atrocity of all this is that they have taken God and sold him. They have taken redemption and sold it. They have taken spirituality and sold it.

They just don't sell things, they take things. The Church appropriates things for itself—just about everything. It has claimed apostolic succession, degrees of sin (The biggest sin, mortal sin, is not going to its clubhouse every Sunday), the idea that it is the only true church and the only path to God, the idea of papal infallibility for the entire Christian world, indulgences, the body and blood of Christ, the law unto itself—you name it, they've appropriated it.

It's like a bully on a playground. That swing set has been there for years and was built for everyone, but the bully, meaning the Catholic Church, claims it for itself. "Those swings are ours," it says, "so is the sandbox and the monkey bars and the see-saw and the slides. You can't use this playground or any of the equipment unless you join our club and pledge your mind, heart, soul and children to us and give us your total subservience and a good portion of your money."

Where does that leave the rest of us?

What I'm saying is that the playground and the sandbox and the slides and the swings don't belong just to them. Nor does God and redemption.

The word "Catholic" is derived from the Greek word "katholikos," which means "universal."

To Catholic Church officers, universal includes child rapists. It excludes anyone who has been raped by one of their priests, anyone who has sued them and anyone who challenges their authority.

Look Behind the Curtain

Things become clear to us and we can act accordingly on that clarity once we look behind the curtain of deceit, arrogance, lies, fake humility and piety, and the lust for power, authority, money and control.

In some ways, the Church has handled this rapist-priests situation masterfully. It has given lip service to the problem, the pope has admitted the problem and promised, who knows what, and he has met with some rape victims and cried.

What an insult. Give me action instead of tears from the pope, who, by the way, is nothing but a guy in a dress, a silly-looking hat and silk slippers. Give me a sincere, humble and anguished contrition instead of tears. Give me change—a total change of leadership and management instead of tears. Give me a policy of turning the rapists over to authorities instead of tears. Give me truth, honesty, justice, dignity and true repentance instead of tears. Give me a sincere apology and request for my forgiveness instead of tears. Give me an unshakable vow that this will never again happen to another child—ever—and give me a loophole-free policy to back it up.

Instead of tears and teams of lawyers and thousands of pages of Canon Law and ecclesiastical statements, papal pronouncements, more dogma, masses for the victims, cover-ups, corruption, contempt for and continued legal and spiritual abuse of the victims and half-hearted attempts to appease victims that are designed to ensure that this will all go away and be forgotten—that things will return to normal and that those in power remain in power—instead of all of that, give me kindness, caring and love for the masses. Give me the idea that those bureaucrats are not better or holier or on a higher plane than we are and that your managers don't matter more than we do.

Give me an end to the bureaucracy, the destruction of its palaces, and the idea that those bureaucrats need to get real jobs. Do any of them actually work? Do any of them do anything other than scare people into giving them their money?

Give me Christ-like behavior.

I won't hold my breath.

****

Christ-like behavior also means getting angry and challenging arrogance, power and self-serving, abusive authority.

To paraphrase Tom Doyle, Jesus was a revolutionary. The only time he really got angry was when he went into temples and churches and saw the power, the abuse, the arrogance, the hypocrisy and the denigration of human beings by those in religious power and authority. He got pissed when those in religious authority tried every scheme they could to get people's money.

Yeah, Christ got angry. He wasn't a dupe. Christ was not a wimp. He studied. He talked. He understood. He got angry. He challenged. He threw his fists, and he threw them without restraint and without fear. He pulled no punches. He stood up to and he challenged the religious powers, authorities and bureaucracies of his time. He told them they were full of shit. He never preached that you had to go through a priest to talk to God. He cared about people, not about power.

You should too. You should get angry—no, make that pissed, furious and outraged and motivated to stop giving your allegiance and money to an organization that protects child rapists—about the fact that more than 5,700 priests in the U.S. alone have been credibly accused of molesting and raping children and adults. There are estimates that the set-tlements have cost the organization in the U.S. between $1 billion and $3 billion.

That could have built a lot of roofs, playgrounds, paid a lot of teachers, and, more importantly, bought so much food for so many hungry people. Instead, so much of it went to lawyers.

Much of that money went to lawyers who tried mightily to denigrate people who have been raped by Catholic priests. Can you imagine that? Your people hired lawyers to fuck with children who have been raped by priests. Do you support that? Would you spend your money that way? Do you approve of the money you put into those baskets and plates on Sundays to go to lawyers who trash people who've been raped by priests?

If you do, let me remind you again. The fat, smelly, hairy, flabby, stinky, smoking, boozing, shit-encrusted-ass Smith told me that God sanctioned—naah—that God demanded that he stick his dick up my fifteen-year-old ass and that I never tell anyone about it, lest he get my younger brothers.

Would you give him your money? Would you let him near your son or daughter or niece or nephew? Would you support with your hearts, minds, bodies and souls an organization that protects even one child rapist?

When you sit in those pews and give the Church your money, that's what you are doing.

If you don't complain, don't demand immediate change and don't demand that the child-raping monsters be turned over for prosecution, then, well, you are criminals and rapists yourselves.

****

The thing that has sickened me and driven me crazy all these years is that Church officials just don't care. No, they do care. They care about themselves, their image, their power, their authority, their privilege and our money. They really do believe that they're better, smarter and holier than we are.

This was all really simple and they could have saved a few billion bucks.

All they needed to do from the beginning was turn the rapists—each and every one of them—over to civil authorities for prosecution. That would have made it clear from the beginning all those centuries ago that rapist priests would never be tolerated. They could have apologized to every rape victim, gotten them help, asked for their forgiveness and put concrete policies in place to ensure that no child or adult would ever again be sexually molested or raped by one of their priests.

It was simple, but they never did it.

Instead, they enabled all those raping pigs. They told them that they were better than us by saying they were priestly, kingly people and God's chosen ones. They told them they were successors to the apostles. Imagine what that does to a person's mind, especially a young mind that is still developing.

Can you imagine what went on in those sick minds? They gave them God's authority to act on their beastly urges. They unlocked the cages for those guys, let them out and then continued to feed their beasts. They slapped their wrists—a lot of times they didn't even do that—and then they transferred them around and gave them more children to rape.

They didn't just fail us children and our parents and relatives and friends, and when we became adults, our children and spouses. They failed those priests as well. They were sick and they needed to get well. In the case of rape, that includes punishment. Instead of giving them medicine, the Catholic Church gave them poison.

They failed everyone.

Don't they shudder in fear about that? I would.

The pope, I'm sorry, the Church's CEO, says the organization and its members need to do penance. If they want to do penance, they should read this book and all the others about their vile rapists and cover-ups, and they should live every day with this shit that we've had to deal with. Live our pain, sorrow, humiliation and shame. Live our torment, and live it every day.

Better yet, they should pray and ask God to take all of our torment and give it to themselves. They should relieve us of our pain by taking it on themselves. They must take it on for all those people whose lives they've ruined for all these thousands of years.

They should do this: Read scripture. Dump their Canon Law and ecclesiastical statements and *ex cathedra* proclamations. They should lock them in a room and go on a retreat and take only the Bible. They'll get the answers they need really quick because they're right there.

Unlike their Canon Law and self-serving pronouncements, scripture doesn't and hasn't changed. They'll be able to follow it. They won't be confused and befuddled and wonder from one day to the next whether they're out of conformity with regulations because they suddenly changed again.

Scripture is simple and direct. It says love one another, not rape one another. It says protect the children, not the guys who raped them. It says be fair and just, not a haven for criminals. It says live a good life and be kind and simple, not build a giant bureaucracy to write incomprehensible and contradictory rules and regulations to control people and take their money. It says do unto others as you would have them do unto you.

By protecting the child rapists, I have to figure that they would want that to happen to them. I figure they too want to be raped and have their rapist roam unfettered so they can rape and rape and rape again.

****

I've written this book so I can start healing, and in the hopes that it will cause people, especially Catholics, to rise up angry and demand with an unrelenting fury of Church officials that never again—ever—will a child or anyone else be sexually abused and raped by one of their priests. That never again will a child be sacrificed on their altars of lust, power, greed, arrogance, image, privilege and lies.

That is what has happened. They have engaged in the practice of offering human sacrifices, and their victims have been children.

To all you Catholics out there I say this:

Will you continue to be part of an organization that has offered up children as human sacrifices? If a corporation offered up children as human sacrifices, would you not be outraged? Would you not demand justice and punishment? Would you not demand that the corporation's officials who contributed to and encouraged those human sacrifices be thrown in prison to rot?

What if it was your child or niece or nephew or neighbor who was offered up as a human sacrifice? Would you be sick? Would you fly into a blinding rage and demand justice and change? Would you be outraged enough to storm the company's headquarters and shout so the entire world could hear:

"Die fuckers! No more, and never again. Ever!"

Would you not want to drag the perpetrators out of their plush offices and tear them apart piece by piece and limb by limb?

Your church offered up me and thousands upon thousands of other children as human sacrifices to their rapist priests. Are you not outraged enough to storm the Vatican and drag those pigs out of their gilded palaces into St. Peter's Square and tear them apart?

Should not their gold be melted and their priceless paintings and plush appointments and costly vestments and marble statues and golden staffs be sold to care for the poor, the sick, the homeless and the hungry?

There is one thing that has kept me going through this horror and this torment for thirty-eight years. That is the thought that vengeance is not mine. It is God's.

I can't understand why Catholic Church officials are not just a little bit afraid.

"If your church had practiced what it preaches, if it had demanded of itself what it demands of us, if it had acted Christlike, well, guess what? No kid would ever have been raped by a 'man of God.'"—Larry Monte Jr.

Twenty

Healing

Dear All Who've Been Raped by Catholic Priests:

I start the end with an apology and a trembling request for forgiveness from my wife and my children and from everyone who has been sexually molested or raped by a Catholic priest.

I am late to this. I had an opportunity in the early 1990s to take on the Catholic Church and its raping priests and its bishops, archbishops, cardinals and popes who protected and enabled them to rape and rape and rape more children.

I didn't jump at that opportunity to fight for justice and for all of those who had been so horribly abused and degraded by the Church. I ran from it. I wanted nothing to do with the lawsuits. I continued to keep the Church's vile secrets. In doing so, I was an accessory to any molestation and rape by a priest that occurred after I got that phone call from those lawyers asking me to join their lawsuit.

I lied to the lawyers when I said that I had not been raped by Smith. I lied to my wife when she asked about the phone call and about newspaper articles saying Smith had been sued as a rapist. I lied to my brothers. I lied to my sisters and other relatives. I lied and lied and lied some more.

I was, I admit, a slave and selfish. I still believed totally in the Catholic Church and everything it taught. I wanted no harm to come to the Church, and I wanted no harm or further shame to come to me.

When I did contact the Santa Fe archdiocese, I asked for a personal apology. It was about me. It wasn't about all the others. It wasn't about the shocking, pervasive and systemic criminality and its cover-up. It was about me: Larry.

My lies and my refusal to confront my guilt and shame and to confront my abusers hurt everyone around me. In that way, I abused them.

All of you, please, please, forgive me. I beg of you, forgive me. Forgive me my fear, my shame, my lies and my silence. Forgive me my blind acceptance of, and slavish adherence to everything the Catholic Church stood for, said and did. I too protected the rapists.

No more, though, and never again.

I am standing tall and swinging back, not just for myself, but for everyone whose lives have been ruined by the Catholic Church and its raping priests.

****

I also need to say this. This has been more than two hundred pages of unrelenting screaming, but my life has not been just that.

I've been married for thirty years to the most wonderful and incredible woman on the earth, Jean. She has saved my life so many times. You do remember that Smith told me not to marry her. He said that if I did, the marriage would last only two years.

Fuck Smith, and fuck all those priests, bishops, cardinals and popes. Fuck them all.

We have five wonderful and incredible children.

I've been a success in business, despite this shit. In many ways, I have already conquered it.

I've had good fellowship and good friends and many—so many—damn good times. Oh! I have had such good scotch and good conversation with such wonderful and caring friends! I have had too many laughs to count.

Life has not just been me walking around every day with my head down, shoulders slouched and mumbling an endless stream of profanities.

Life has often been good.

But in the back, and some days, in the forefront, and in the sides of my mind, this shit has always been there. It always will. I'm hoping that I can now let other things, instead of a nagging torment and anger and rage and shame and humiliation, fill my mind.

****

This journey of going from slave to doubter to beginning to heal and to finally fighting back began in earnest in 2002 after I got that letter from Sheehan. That's the "we're from the order of Melchizedek and can't be fired" letter of July 19 of that year. I fumed and raged and continued to withdraw and hurt myself.

It was in September of 2006 that I tried to hang myself with belts secured to a doorknob and when Jean found me banging my head against wall of our house on our upstairs balcony. That ended with my first visit to Kaseman Hospital. That was a warning sign, but not a big enough one for me.

October 13, 2006, was my day of reckoning. That's when I began to truly start healing. That was the day I picked up the telephone in my shop and heard Sheehan calling for my dad. I stayed on the line and heard that pig say once again that all the rapes had occurred thirty years prior, that it wasn't his fault and that he had cleaned things up.

I could no longer deal with the lies. That's when I stumbled out back to the alley behind the shop and sat down and burned my hands and my arms with a cigar and banged my head into a metal door.

That landed me straight into Kaseman's psych ward, laced into a straitjacket, pumped full of sedatives, put into a room with bars on the window, strapped to the rails of my bed and given crayons and a coloring book to play with. It was the most humiliating thing that had ever happened to me. They say you have to hit rock bottom in order to heal, and that was my bottom.

From there I went to The Meadows in Wickenburg, Arizona, for thirty days. I needed more and longer-term treatment, and I would have gone for ninety days had not my father's cancer returned.

I'm now getting therapy from the good doctor Reinhart Schelert. He is helping me see that the rapes weren't my fault, that I no longer need to own shame and guilt and that I have to accept that this happened to me but that it doesn't define me.

I am Larry Monte, a loving and devoted husband, a damn good (despite my problems) and loving father, successful businessman, friend, and good guy. I care about people. I am kind. I give of myself and I try every day to live Christ's teachings: Love one another and do unto others as you would have them do unto you.

Most importantly, at least at this point, I am no longer a slave to the Catholic Church. I am free, independent and unafraid to speak my mind and seek the truth. I don't need the Catholic Church for redemption and salvation. I no longer need its apology. I no longer need the Church for personal validation. I need myself, my family and God for that.

Things are getting better for me. I realize that the Catholic Church will never sincerely apologize to me or to us and that it will never ask for our forgiveness. I have come to recognize that the Catholic Church's leadership is evil and that it won't change for a long time, if ever at all.

I know now that priests can and do commit vile and evil acts. I know that priests are not better than me or anyone else. I know they are not my or anyone's link to God. I know that they are not holier than me or anyone else. I know that the Catholic Church makes up rules to control people and makes them up anytime it wants.

Here is what I have also learned through this horrible journey, and I hope this will help any priest sexual abuse victim, hell, any sexual abuse victim who has yet to seek help.

You have to get psychological help and therapy immediately. Your mind, your spirit and your soul have been wounded. Broken, really.

Think of it like my busted up ankle after I fell off that ladder. My leg was cracked in two and bone was sticking through my skin. That was a wound, and because it was physical and visible, not to mention stunningly painful, I went to a hospital and got it fixed.

Trauma of all kinds wounds the brain and the spirit. We don't think of it as a wound because we can't see it. The damage is as severe, though, as a cracked bone or a heart attack or a severe gash or a cracked skull. Your mind has been wounded and you need to fix and heal it.

Think also of that year in which my leg didn't heal. The wound split and stayed open and it oozed and it bled and it hurt and it was awful.

A traumatized mind that is not getting psychological and spiritual help does the same thing. It fails to heal, and for years and years it oozes and bleeds and hurts.

You know the symptoms: the daily anguish, depression, shame, guilt, boozing, self-mutilation, self-loathing, constant anger, rage, tantrums, vandalism, and on and on. They are symptoms. Do not sweep them under the rug and think that things will get better on their own or that you'll heal yourself. You can't and you won't. Think of it as a busted leg or a clogged artery. The leg must be set to heal properly, and an artery has to be unclogged and scraped clean. Let that leg heal on its own and you'll have a deformed leg and be a gimp.

A wound to the brain and psyche requires the same kind of professional care.

And consider this if you haven't yet gotten professional help:

Do you want to wind up in prison? On the street and homeless? In a psych ward? In an early grave? Do you want your children or your relatives or spouse to come home one day and see you hanging from a door by a belt around your neck? Do you want your kids to grow up despising and hating you because you're a drunken, raging, furniture-throwing monster?

Those things will happen if you don't get professional help.

Consider this as well:

Do you want to be pissed off and angry all the time, or do you want to be happy and live a life of joy and peace and laughter and love?

I'm guessing you want the latter. Why wait to get it? Why wait thirty-eight years like I did? Why miss out on all of life's good things?

Understand that it is a dark cloud that envelopes you. Know, though, that it will be permanent only if you let it. You can step out of the darkness of shame and guilt and feelings of being defective and into the light of joy, hope, love and confidence.

Get help now! Live a life of joy and happiness and confidence and love now!

For god sakes, though, whatever you do, do not go to the Catholic Church for help. They will demean, brutalize and shame you again. Never ever go to the Catholic Church for help.

To those whose family members have been raped by priests, understand that they have been wounded and hurt to their very core and that they can't "just get over it." That is the most vile, disgusting, hurtful and demeaning thing you can say to someone who has been sexually abused. Their souls, their spirits and their minds have been shattered.

Understand that every moment of every day they hear voices that tell them they are not worthy of anything, including life itself; that they hear voices that tell them they are guilty and are full of shame and are defective to the core. Understand that every day they berate and blame themselves for what happened to them.

Understand that they need help that you can't give them. Help them get to a shrink.

Whatever you do, always be kind and gentle and loving. It will be difficult, but please do it. Your loved one has been brutalized to a point that you can never comprehend. Their mind is like an open, oozing, bleeding and throbbing wound.

****

I did not want to write this book. I've had to relive this crap all over again and it made me physically and emotionally ill. Writing this and reliving this was the last thing I ever wanted to do. I'd love to be writing about anything else. I had to write it in order to start healing and to try to shout down the Catholic Church and its lies. We can no longer let this institution destroy people.

I leave you with this from Paul's letter to the Corinthians:

"If I speak in human and angelic tongues, but do not have love, I am a resounding gong or a clashing cymbal. And if I have the gift of prophecy and comprehend all mysteries and all knowledge; if I have all faith so as to move mountains but do not have love, I am nothing. If I give away everything I own, and if I hand my body over so that I may boast but do not have love, I gain nothing.

"Love is patient, love is kind. It is not jealous, it is not pompous it is not inflated. It is not rude and it does not seek its own interests, it is not quick-tempered and it does not brood over injury, it does not rejoice over wrongdoing, but rejoices with the truth. It bears all things, believes all things, hopes all things, endures all things.

"Love never fails. If there are prophecies they will be brought to nothing, if tongues they will cease; if knowledge it will be brought to nothing. For we know partially and we prophesy partially, but when the perfect comes, the partial will pass away.

"When I was a child, I used to talk as a child, think as a child, reason as a child, when I became a man, I put aside childish things. At present we see indistinctly, as in a mirror, but then face to face. At present I know partially, then I shall know fully, as I am fully known.

"So faith, hope, love remain, these three; but the greatest of these is love."

****

I'm done.

Now I'm going to do something I haven't done in thirty-eight years.

I'm off for a little while to cry.

With joy,

Larry

www.ingramcontent.com/pod-product-compliance
Lightning Source LLC
LaVergne TN
LVHW011220080426
835509LV00005B/225